What People Are Sa
Chicken Soup for the Gr

"Mark and Jack have done it again! One of the most difficult aspects of the experience we call 'grief' is the sense that we are alone, isolated, separate. . . . This wonderful collection of heart-warming, heart-opening stories will nurture you, inspire you and help you to heal. They will help you to know that you are not alone . . . that all of us—the entire human family—share in the experience of loss, sadness and disappointment. But we can NEVER lose the love in our hearts. Each experience of loss can be a doorway to deeper and deeper levels of love, peace, healing and—ultimately—joy! In the midst of inevitable change we can find that which is never lost and never changes . . . our true heart. Love never dies."

John E. Welshons
author, *Awakening from Grief: Finding the Road Back to Joy*

"What a celebration of love and life! Whether you are grieving the loss of a loved one, looking to comfort a grieving friend or searching for hope and inspiration, you'll be able to find it in *Chicken Soup for the Grieving Soul.* This book shows us that no life is without meaning and no story of grief written without caring, compassionate love. It is filled with heartwarming, inspirational and uplifting stories that will bring a tear to your eye and a smile to your lips while soothing the grieving soul."

Patricia Loder
executive director, The Compassionate Friends, Inc.

"Once again, Jack Canfield and Mark Victor Hansen take us on a journey of the heart. Even if you are not presently dealing with grief, these stories will move you and remind you of what really matters in your life. It's times like these that open our hearts and lead us back into loving arms."

Kenny Loggins
musician/author

"Very much like a meaningful funeral that honors the life of someone we love, Jack Canfield and Mark Victor Hansen's collection of stories reaffirms that every life has meaning and that by sharing one's grief with others, it allows us to become stronger."

Joe Weigel
director of communications, Batesville Casket Company

"Like having a talk with wise, caring and compassionate friends, this invaluable resource both gently and powerfully guides the reader through the journey of mourning, healing and hope. I cannot recommend it highly enough."

Rabbi Earl A. Grollman, D.H.L., D.D.
author, *Living When a Loved One Has Died*

"*Chicken Soup for the Grieving Soul* is a handbook of hope and healing that not only teaches friends and family members how to help loved ones during their time of loss, it also offers stories with such powerful take-away messages for the one in pain that it will change the way we grieve forever. This is one of those books that should be stockpiled in your home to place lovingly into the hands of everyone who experiences the death of a loved one. The tears you shed while reading this book will soothe your soul and, without a doubt, help you become a better person."

Patricia Lorenz
one of America's most prolific
Chicken Soup for the Soul writers

"Grieving can be a bridge to our experiencing a spiritual transformation. It can help us look at our own fears about death and separation and consider the possibility that we are eternal spiritual beings who are only temporary in bodies. There is no school for grieving and facing the loss of a loved one. Unfortunately, many of our cultures do not encourage us to face our feelings about death and loss, to be honest and open about honoring our human experience, and to use our grieving experiences as part of our spiritual growth. The stories in this book are medicine for healing the grieving heart and freeing the soul."

Gerald Jampolsky, M.D.
Diane V. Cirincione, Ph.D.
Center for Attitudinal Healing, Sausalito, California

CHICKEN SOUP
FOR THE
GRIEVING SOUL

Chicken Soup for the Grieving Soul
Stories About Life, Death and Overcoming the Loss of a Loved One
Jack Canfield, Mark Victor Hansen

Published by Backlist, LLC,
a unit of Chicken Soup for the Soul Publishing, LLC. www.chickensoup.com

Front cover artwork by Larissa Hise Henoch
Originally published in 2003 by Health Communications, Inc.

Back cover and spine redesign by Pneuma Books, LLC

Distributed to the booktrade by Simon & Schuster. SAN: 200-2442

Publisher's Cataloging-in-Publication Data
(Prepared by The Donohue Group)

Chicken soup for the grieving soul : stories about life, death and
overcoming the loss of a loved one / [compiled by] Jack Canfield [and]
Mark Victor Hansen.

p. : ill. ; cm.

Originally published: Deerfield Beach, FL : Health Communications, c2003.
ISBN: 978-1-62361-101-9

1. Bereavement--Anecdotes. 2. Anecdotes. I. Canfield, Jack, 1944- II.
Hansen, Mark Victor.

BF575.G7 C465 2012
155.9/37   2012944865

PRINTED IN THE UNITED STATES OF AMERICA
on acid free paper

23   13

CHICKEN SOUP FOR THE GRIEVING SOUL

Stories About Life, Death and Overcoming the Loss of a Loved One

Jack Canfield
Mark Victor Hansen

Backlist, LLC, a unit of
Chicken Soup for the Soul Publishing, LLC
Cos Cob, CT
www.chickensoup.com

Contents

3. COPING AND HEALING

4. THOSE WE WILL MISS

5. SPECIAL MOMENTS

6. INSIGHTS AND LESSONS

7. LIVING AGAIN

Introduction

When we mourn the loss of someone we love, it feels like no one in the world can understand what we are going through—the pain, the agony, the overwhelming loss. *Chicken Soup for the Grieving Soul* is our gift to those who are brokenhearted. Some of the greatest rewards for us in producing *Chicken Soup* books are the letters we receive from our readers telling us how our stories have impacted their lives. Literally thousands of people have reported finding comfort and healing during their toughest times. It was in response to these hearts and their requests that *Chicken Soup for the Grieving Soul* was created.

A miracle occurs when people bravely write their stories to share with the world. In the process of writing them, they are reconnected with that which they have lost. In the reading of their stories, others are connected to them. And in that connection, everyone feels less alone. Each gains a little more strength for living their life and navigating their way through the challenges and over the hurdles of this journey called grieving.

We offer this collection of true stories as a "support group" of sorts—a place where those suffering a loss can find solace in reading how those in similar, or completely different, situations have handled their grief. These stories are so powerful, so poignant, that you may want to read just one at a sitting and then take time to absorb its message. You will discover that in each story, the thread of hope is woven. Hope for tomorrow. Hope for healing. Hope for once more embracing life and moving on.

Please accept this gift from us and know that we are with you in spirit on this painful yet powerful part of your journey through life.

[EDITORS' NOTE: *Due to our desire to ensure that this collection would include the most comforting stories possible, we have chosen to include a few stories that have appeared in previous volumes of* Chicken Soup for the Soul.]

1

FINAL GIFTS

The best and most beautiful things in the world cannot be seen, nor touched, but are felt in the heart.

Helen Keller

A Timeless Gift

When a door closes . . . look for an open window . . . but it may take a while to feel the breeze.

Anonymous

Emerging from shock after my husband Ken died, I discovered strange things happening around me. Each morning I found doors unlocked, the television blaring and sprinklers spraying. Something shattered my life, and I felt utterly unprotected and vulnerable.

Once I had been a mentally strong, independent woman—handy qualities for a young navy wife living in strange places and rearing four children alone. My husband's ship cruised half a world away, often through hostile waters toward secret destinations. The possibility that he might not make it back was never far from my mind. After all that experience living apart in the early years of our marriage, I now wondered if I had what it took to live alone.

A friend's words helped me understand what I was feeling. "You lost someone you love, and nothing has prepared you for what happens next. You're reacting to intense pain by closing down and buying time to heal. You still function," she said, "but now you are operating on automatic. And don't forget, nobody is doing your husband's chores."

Ken had efficiently taken care of making my world safe by quietly fixing, renewing or replacing what needed to be done. In my current state of mind, if I remembered to turn anything on, I usually forgot to disconnect it, taking for granted that what needed to run, sprinkle or turn off would do so on its own.

As friends and relatives gradually drifted back into their own routines, I stayed home, stared off into space and withdrew from life. It was obvious I needed help, but it was easier to do nothing, live in the past and feel sorry for myself.

Moving forward was hard, and I looked for excuses not to try. Day after day I prayed for guidance. Finally, one Sunday about two months after Ken died, the church bulletin included an announcement for the beginning of a new grief-recovery workshop. One statement caught my attention: "Grief is real, powerful and has a devastating impact on our ability to function." The class started in two days. *This must be an answer to prayer,* I thought, so I followed God's direction and signed up. It felt right to be in his hands.

My confidence wavered as I walked to the first session. It was more difficult than I ever imagined. I felt as though I wore a sign saying, "No spouse! All alone! Abandoned!"

Beginning with that first night, the seven members in my group empathized with each other's tragic loss as our bonding included advice from the heart, the hand of friendship and a sympathetic ear. Joining this group was the first step I had taken to help myself and one that would eventually make me feel better, stronger and less vulnerable.

Our homework assignment? Do something pleasurable for ourselves. I splurged on new plum-colored sheets, transforming "our" bedroom into "my" room with a cheerful, feminine décor. Then, because I never owned one before, I bought a navy blue designer baseball cap. Checking out the hat, I glanced in the mirror and smiled. Being good to myself could easily become a habit.

Facilitators cautioned us about letting painful reminders of the dead person stay in our lives. Guilt can lure us into making our homes a shrine to their memory. I called mine "the recliner shrine." Grandchildren's crayon drawings, an old newspaper and a mug inscribed "Dad's Cup" remained where he left them on a small table beside the recliner.

The chair's emptiness served as a constant reminder that he was gone. My children looked for Dad in his favorite place each time they entered the room. It was just too painful, so they took action. They reorganized the house. Immobilized by his death and still too stunned to move, I sat in the rocker and watched them work. Couches and chairs, followed by end tables, lamps and pictures, all ended up in a new spot or a different room. I loved the way it looked. The recliner, hidden under a floral cover, was relocated to an inconspicuous corner of the house, still with us, but no longer a blatant reminder.

Grief facilitators taught me how to face the finality of my partner's death. I realized that grieving is not a place for me to stay, nor can I go back, for my old life is no longer there. Accepting that it's all right for me to survive is a big part of healing.

In addition, facilitators admonished each week, "Take care of yourself." Since my husband was no longer here to make my world safe, I would do it myself. Using a twelve-point system, I secured the house, counting each job: (1) lock the door; (2) close the windows; (3) turn off the TV, etc. If I reached my bed with less than twelve, I knew I had missed a room and had to start over. Counting brought me security and peace of mind.

I resolved to simplify and reorganize my life. Feeling easily distracted and maddeningly forgetful, I bought a monthly planner that I kept in full view on the kitchen counter. I made a do, buy or be list: *Do* call plumber, wash car, *buy* milk and bread, *be* at vet 4 P.M. (don't forget the dog). This visual reminder lessened the stress of trying to remember everything.

On the first-year anniversary of my husband's death, I filled a basket with strawberries, pears, grapes, plums and other colorful fruits. Then I attached a note of appreciation and delivered it to the hospital intensive-care staff. I had been too devastated before to thank them for such compassionate care of both patient and family.

My daughter asked, "You're not doing a shrine thing again, are you?"

"No," I promised, "these gifts are to nourish the living, so they can continue helping others in need."

Later that day while emptying my husband's desk, I found a torn piece of paper from an artist's Morilla sketchbook. The unexpected note was not dated, but I recognized Ken's handwriting immediately. "Dearest wife and children, Forgot to tell you how much I love you—I do." My eyes filled with grateful tears.

Ken always said things happened for a reason. This gift that arrived without a date on the anniversary of his death was very special. It reminded me that I was loved deeply, I loved him in return, and our love became part of us forever—even when one left and the other moved toward a new life alone. Eventually, the pain of parting diminishes, but the love remains forever—like a timeless gift.

Gloria Givens

A Rose for Mother

With garden resurrections every year,
Life after death is not so queer.

Agnes Ryan

Sometimes, when sorrow is deep and the healing balm of time moves too slowly, a grieving heart may look for consolation in something more tangible. When I lost my mother, the comfort I sought depended on the survival of a single rose. Nothing could have prepared me for the answer I received.

My husband and I are avid rose growers. When we joined a local rose society, we became involved in rose competitions where hundreds of blooms of every color and variety are judged for trophies. Growing show roses takes a great deal of time and energy, but the garden was our haven where we gladly retreated into a world of sunshine and beauty.

My mother also loved our yard, and each time she came to our home, she would soon disappear into the garden. I often teased her about wanting to visit with the roses more than with us. She had been struggling with progressive kidney failure, and the garden was where she went to recover after her exhausting dialysis treatments. When she was strong enough, she would roam through the pathways inspecting and clipping her way around the bushes, since it was her self-appointed mission to fill the house with beautiful bouquets. Eventually, when she became too ill to walk through the garden, she was content to sit in the shade surrounded by the flowers and birds. By the end of summer she had grown very frail, and with a heavy heart I knew this would be her last summer in the garden.

An unpredictable complication sent her into a coma, and she suddenly passed away two days before Christmas. After the funeral, I went into the garden hoping to find some comfort in the place she had loved so much. I was searching for a sense of her spirit among the roses, but the garden was in its dormant stage and the barrenness matched the emptiness I felt in my heart.

The following day, some friends from church brought us a new rosebush in her memory. They had selected one called Dainty Bess, a beautiful five-petal rose in cotton-candy pink with dark red stamens and a soft, sweet smell. It would be a lovely reminder of Mother. We planted the rosebush near the place where she had spent so many peaceful hours, and for me the bush became a symbol of her ongoing spirit. I spent the winter months pampering the little plant, urging it to survive and grow strong.

The cold rains finally stopped, and an early spring transformed our yard into a riot of fragrant color. Mother would have loved it, and I missed sharing her joy and enthusiasm for the garden.

Dainty Bess was thriving, covered with bright green leaves and, to our surprise, five long-stemmed buds. When the first delicate bloom opened, my spirits soared for the first time in months.

Our first rose show was five days away, and I became determined to enter a Dainty Bess bloom in memory of my mother's life, believing this would finally put an end to my grieving. Unusually warm weather had quickly opened three of the five buds, so I cut the last two and placed them in the refrigerator to slow the blooming process. The day before the show, I tried to force them open by putting them in warm water. The first bud refused to open and simply bowed its head, but the last one was perfect. I placed it back in the refrigerator and prayed it would survive. Later that day, a nagging fear of losing the rose sent me out to the garden hoping to find another Dainty Bess hiding among the leaves, but there was no sign of a bud anywhere.

The next morning I opened up the refrigerator to find a bare stem in the vase and five pink petals lying on the shelf! I burst into tears. Losing the rose suddenly brought back all the memories of losing my mother. My husband gave me a comforting hug. "We'll enter a Dainty Bess at the next show," he said soothingly. But I could hear the disappointment in his voice.

With heavy hearts, we went into the garden to check the rest of the rosebushes for last-minute blooms before leaving for the show. Barely glancing at the Dainty Bess bush as I walked by, a small splash of color caught my eye. My gasp of surprise brought Rich rushing over to see what was wrong, and together we stared in disbelief at a single long-stemmed, tightly folded bud in the center of the bush. Faith had taught me to believe in miracles, but this was beyond all understanding. Almost afraid to touch it, I finally cut the stem. In stunned silence, we drove to the show.

When we arrived at the exhibit hall, the bud had barely begun to unfurl. I polished the leaves, then cupped my hands over the bloom and gave it several warm puffs of my breath to encourage it to open. I knew the rose would be disqualified if the petals weren't fully opened by the time it was judged.

After I had done all I could, I stood back and looked at the little rose. Its beauty was breathtaking. Its half-opened petals reaching upward reminded me that I had been blessed with an extraordinary act of compassion. Then I realized that my competitive spirit had momentarily blinded me to the real reason for showing this rose—not for the prize or the glory of winning, but to honor my mother's life. The rose was perfect just the way it was, and the judge's opinion was no longer relevant. With a grateful heart and a sense of reverence, I placed the rose on the display table and walked away, free at last from sorrow's grip.

When the judging was completed, we rushed over to retrieve our special rose. It had disappeared from the table! Seeing our confusion, a friend came over and asked if we had looked on the trophy table. There it was—opened to perfection, draped with a blue ribbon and standing next to a large silver trophy that said "Best Single-Petal Rose in Show." It was a beautiful and unexpected tribute to my mother.

A few days later, I pressed the rose, hoping to keep it forever as proof that miracles do happen. But when I checked it just one week later, it had disintegrated into a fine powder that scattered into the air as I unfolded the paper around it. The rose had come into my life to console my aching heart, then vanished as mysteriously as it had appeared once its work was done.

Maria E. Sears

Mom's Last Laugh

Some orthodox member of Thoreau's family asked him if he had made his peace with God. Only Thoreau could have answered as he did, that he was not aware that he and God had ever quarreled.

Source Unknown

Consumed by my loss, I didn't notice the hardness of the pew where I sat. I was at the funeral of my dearest friend, my mother. She finally had lost her long battle with cancer. The hurt was so intense that I found it hard to breathe at times.

Always supportive, Mother clapped loudest at my school plays, held a box of tissues while listening to my first heartbreak, comforted me at my father's death, encouraged me in college and prayed for me my entire life.

At the time Mother's illness was diagnosed, my sister was caring for a new baby and my brother had recently married, so it fell to me, the twenty-seven-year-old middle child without entanglements, to take care of her. I considered it an honor.

"What now, Lord?" I asked sitting in church. My life stretched out before me like an abyss.

My brother sat stoically with his face toward the cross while clutching his wife's hand. My sister sat slumped against her husband's shoulder, his arms around her as she cradled their child. They were all so deeply grieving that no one noticed I sat alone.

My place had been with our mother, preparing her meals, helping her walk, taking her to the doctor, seeing to her medication and reading the Bible together. Now she was with the Lord.

My work was finished, and I was alone.

I heard a door open and slam shut at the back of the church. Quick footsteps hurried along the carpeted floor. An exasperated young man looked around briefly and then sat next to me. He folded his hands and placed them on his lap. His eyes were brimming with tears. He began to sniffle.

"I'm late," he explained, though no explanation was necessary.

After several eulogies, he leaned over and asked, "Why do they keep calling Mary by the name of Margaret?"

"Because that was her name, Margaret. Never Mary. No one called her Mary," I whispered. I wondered why this person couldn't have sat on the other side of the church. He interrupted my grieving with his tears and fidgeting. Who was this stranger anyway?

"No, that isn't correct," he insisted as several people glanced over at us. He whispered, "Her name is Mary, Mary Peters."

"That isn't who that is."

"Isn't this the Lutheran church?"

"No, the Lutheran church is across the street."

"Oh."

"I believe you're at the wrong funeral, sir."

The solemnness of the occasion mixed with the realization of the man's mistake bubbled out of me as laughter. I cupped my hands over my face, hoping it would be interpreted as sobs.

The creaking pew gave me away. Sharp looks from other mourners only made the situation seem more hilarious. I peeked at the bewildered, misguided man seated beside me. He was laughing, too, as he glanced around, deciding it was too late for an uneventful exit. I imagined Mother laughing.

At the final "Amen," we darted out a door and into the parking lot.

"I do believe we'll be the talk of the town," he smiled. He said his name was Rick and, since he had missed his aunt's funeral, he asked me out for a cup of coffee.

That afternoon began a lifelong journey with this man who attended the wrong funeral, but was in the right place. A year after our meeting, we were married at a country church where he was the assistant pastor. This time we both arrived at the right church, and right on time.

In my time of sorrow, God gave me laughter. In place of loneliness, God gave me love. This past June we celebrated our twenty-third wedding anniversary.

Whenever anyone asks us how we met, Rick tells them, "Her mother and my Aunt Mary introduced us."

Robin Lee Shope

I'm Okay, Mom and Dad

Perhaps they are not the stars, but rather openings in heaven where the love of our lost ones pours through and shines down upon us to let us know they are happy.

Inspired by an Eskimo Legend

When I returned home from the funeral of a church member, my grown daughter, Jenny, asked me about the service. I had been very moved by a story the priest told about a dragonfly, so I shared it with Jen.

A group of water bugs was talking one day about how they saw other water bugs climb up a lily pad and disappear from sight. They wondered where the other bugs could have gone. They promised one another that if one of them ever went up the lily pad and disappeared, it would come back and tell the others where it had gone.

About a week later one of the water bugs climbed up the lily pad and emerged on the other side. As it sat there, it transformed into a dragonfly. Its body took on an iridescent sheen, and four beautiful wings sprouted from its back. The dragonfly flapped its wings and took off in flight, doing loops and spins through the sunlit sky. In the midst of its joyful flight, it remembered the promise it had made to return and tell the other bugs where it had gone. So the dragonfly swooped down to the surface of the water and tried to reenter the water, but try as it would, it could not return.

The dragonfly said to itself, *Well, I tried to keep my promise, but even if I did return, the others wouldn't recognize me in my new glorious body. I guess they will just have to wait until they climb the lily pad to find out where I have gone and what I have become.*

When I had finished relating the short story, my daughter said, with tears running down her cheeks, "Mom, that's really beautiful!" I agreed, and we talked for a while about it.

Two days later, early Sunday morning, July 9, 1995, Jenny came into my room, waking me to say good-bye before leaving for work at a resort on Lake Okoboji. I hugged and kissed her and told her I would see her that night when I joined her for a week's vacation at the lake. I asked her if she had eaten breakfast and if she was wide awake, as we had been out late the night before. I knew she was tired.

"Yes, Mom, I'll see you later!"

Several hours later, our worst nightmare began. Jenny had been involved in a head-on collision and was flown to Sioux Falls, South Dakota. Thoughts crowded in on me: *Why hadn't I fixed her breakfast? Did I tell her I loved her? If I'd kept her with me a few minutes longer, would things have turned out differently? Why hadn't I hugged her a little longer? Why hadn't I kept her home with me that summer instead of letting her work at the lake? Why? Why? Why?*

We flew to Sioux Falls and arrived at noon. Our Jen was hurt mortally, and at ten o'clock that night, she died. If God had given me a choice, I would have traded places with her in a second. Jenny had so much to give this world. She was so bright, beautiful and loving.

On Friday of that week, my husband and I drove to the lake to see family, and we stopped to see where the accident had occurred. I don't remember a lot, but I know I was hysterical trying to figure out what had happened and why.

Leaving the scene of the accident, I asked my husband to take me to a greenhouse, as I needed to be around beautiful flowers. I just couldn't face anyone yet.

Walking to the back of the hothouse, I heard the fluttering of wings as if a bird or hummingbird was hitting the top of the roof. I was looking at a beautiful rose when a beautiful, large dragonfly landed within arm's length of me. I stood there looking at this lovely creature, and I cried. My husband walked in. I looked at him and said, "Jenny is telling us that she's okay." We stood and looked at the lovely dragonfly for a long time, and as we walked out of the hothouse, the dragonfly remained on the rose.

A couple of weeks later, my husband came running into the house telling me to come outside quickly. When I walked out our door, I could not believe what I saw. There were hundreds of dragonflies flying in front of our house and between ours and the neighbor's. I have never seen that many dragonflies at once in town, and the strangest thing about it was that they were only by our house.

There is no way these two experiences were just coincidences. They were more than that. They were messages from Jen.

Each time I see a dragonfly, beautiful memories of my daughter kiss my grieving heart.

Lark Whittemore Ricklefs

Meant to Be

A few years ago, we had a Lab puppy named Blue whom we loved very much. But because everyone in the family spent so much time at work or at school, it soon became obvious Blue wasn't getting the attention and training she needed. It was a difficult decision, but we decided to see if we could find her a better home than we could provide at that time.

I asked around at our church and at work, looking for a special home for Blue. A coworker told me that she had a friend whose old dog had recently died. The family was looking for a puppy. I knew of the family: the husband was named Frank and his wife, Donna, was a Lamaze instructor who worked at a local hospital. Their children, my friend told me, were crazy about dogs and missed their old dog tremendously. It sounded like the perfect place.

I spoke to Donna on the phone, and she was thrilled about taking Blue. I arranged for my husband to deliver the puppy the following day, which was a Friday. Frank gave my husband their address, 412 Adams, and told him that he would be home all day, doing work on the house, so my husband should look for ladders in the front yard.

The next morning, my husband took Blue and set off in the car. Our sad good-byes were lightened by the knowledge that she was going to a wonderful home.

Donna and Frank lived an hour away, on the other side of the nearest big town. My husband found the house; the number 412 was clearly displayed and there was a ladder in the front yard. Taking the puppy in his arms, he went up to the house and knocked on the door. There was no answer. He waited a moment and knocked again.

A man in the next yard called over to him, "Who are you looking for?"

My husband said, "Frank."

"Oh, Frank went to the hospital," he said. "I don't know when he's coming back."

My husband was irked. Frank had said he'd be home all day. Maybe he'd had to give Donna a ride to work at the hospital. But my husband couldn't wait around. He had made appointments for the rest of the day and had to get going. Something of this must have shown on his face, for the man in the next yard said, "What's the problem, young fella?"

My husband explained his predicament and the neighbor offered to keep the puppy at his house until Frank returned. The neighbor had a fenced yard and said it'd be no trouble at all. He was a nice man with dogs of his own, and my husband decided it would be all right. He gave the puppy to the neighbor and left for his appointments.

The following Monday when I returned to work, my co-worker said to me, "Did you change your mind about giving away Blue?"

Surprised, I answered, "No. Why?"

"Well, Donna told me you never delivered her on Friday. They figured you'd had a change of heart when it came time to really say good-bye."

I told her we certainly *had* delivered Blue. I called Donna and told her about the neighbor taking care of Blue until Frank returned.

"But Frank was home all day!" she insisted. "And we haven't heard from any of our neighbors."

What on earth was going on? We finally figured out that my husband had made a wrong turn and had gone to 412 on the next street over. There had been a storm not long before and many people had ladders out to do roof and gutter repairs. Could it possibly be that the man in that house was also named Frank?

My husband and I got into the car and drove over to see what had become of Blue. We saw immediately that that he'd gone one street too far and we knocked on the door of the house where he'd left Blue.

A red-faced man in his sixties answered our knock. When we explained that we were looking for a puppy that had been delivered here last week, the man answered, "Oh, you mean the one that Frank ordered."

Realizing that the man at 412 on this street was also named Frank, we explained the mix-up. The man's face grew somber.

"What's wrong?" I asked. "Is the puppy all right?"

"Oh, the puppy is fine. In fact, I'm sure the puppy is great. But . . . well, I hope you don't want it back," he said seriously. Seeing the question in our eyes, he continued, "When you came with the puppy on Friday, my neighbor Frank was at the hospital. He'd been out in the yard working and had started having chest pains, so his wife took him to the hospital. Frank never did come home. He died of a massive coronary Friday afternoon. It was a terrible shock for his family, and I decided not to bother them until things had settled down a bit. Yesterday, I brought the puppy over and knocked on their door. Frank's eldest daughter came out. I told her that her father had ordered a puppy and since he hadn't been home, that I'd taken delivery on it for him. I said I didn't know what to do with the little dog now that 'things had changed' at their house.

"The daughter just couldn't believe it. She said, 'My father ordered a puppy? This is Dad's puppy?' Then she reached out and I gave her the pup. She hugged that little dog real tight, stuck her face in its fur and just began to cry.

"I wasn't sure what to say, so I just stood there. After a while, she looked up at me and thanked me. She said, 'You don't know what this means to me. I'm so glad to have my father's dog.' The puppy was wiggling around, trying to kiss the daughter any way it could and her face was just lit up with love."

Amazed at the story I turned to my husband, "We can't take Blue back now."

The man nodded in agreement. "Folks, some things are just meant to be. I'd say that puppy is in exactly the right place."

Cindy Midgette

A Surprise Gift for Mother

Death is the end of a lifetime, not the end of a relationship.

Mitch Albom

On Christmas Day, all the joys of close family relationships radiated throughout our parents' home. The smells of roasted turkey, Southern-baked ham and homemade bread hung in the air. Tables and chairs were set up everywhere to accommodate toddlers, teenagers, parents and grandparents. Every room was lavishly decorated. No family member had ever missed Christmas Day with our parents.

Only this year, things were different. Our father had passed away November 26, and this was our first Christmas without him. Mother was doing her best to be the gracious hostess, but I could tell this was especially hard for her. I felt a catch in my throat, and again I wondered if I should give her my planned Christmas gift, or if it had become inappropriate in my father's absence.

A few months earlier I was putting the finishing touches on portraits I had painted of each of my parents. I'd planned to give them as Christmas gifts. This would be a surprise for everyone, as I had not studied art or tried serious painting. Yet there had been an undeniable urge that pushed me relentlessly to do this. The portraits did look like them, but I was still unsure of my painting skill.

While painting one day, I was surprised by a doorbell ring. Quickly putting all my painting materials out of sight, I opened the door. To my astonishment, my father ambled in alone, never before having visited me without my mother. Grinning, he said, "I've missed our early morning talks. You know, the ones we had before you decided to leave me for another man!" I hadn't been married long. Also, I was the only girl and the baby of the family.

Immediately I wanted to show him the paintings, but I was reluctant to ruin his Christmas surprise. Yet something urged me to share this moment with him. After swearing him to secrecy, I insisted he keep his eyes closed until I had the portraits set on easels. "Okay, Daddy. Now you can look!"

He appeared dazed but said nothing. Getting up, he walked closer to inspect them. Then he withdrew to eye them at a distance. I tried to control my stomach flip-flops. Finally, with a tear escaping down one cheek, he mumbled, "I don't believe it. The eyes are so real that they follow you everywhere—and look how beautiful your mother is. Will you let me have them framed?"

Thrilled with his response, I happily volunteered to drop them off the next day at the frame shop. Several weeks passed. Then one night in November the phone rang, and a cold chill numbed my body. I picked up the receiver to hear my husband, a doctor, say, "I'm in the emergency room. Your father has had a stroke. It's bad, but he is still alive."

Daddy lingered in a coma for several days. I went to see

him in the hospital the day before he died. I slipped my hand in his and asked, "Do you know who I am, Daddy?"

He surprised everyone when he whispered, "You're my darling daughter." He died the next day, and it seemed all joy was drained from the lives of my mother and me.

I finally remembered to call about the portrait framing and thanked God my father had gotten a chance to see the pictures before he died. I was surprised when the shopkeeper told me my father had visited the shop, paid for the framing and had them gift wrapped. In our grief, I had no longer planned to give the portraits to my mother.

Even though we had lost the patriarch of our family, everyone assembled on Christmas Day—making an effort to be cheerful. As I looked into my mother's sad eyes and unsmiling face, I decided to give her Daddy's and my gift. As she stripped the paper from the box, I saw her heart wasn't in it. There was a small card inside attached to the pictures.

After looking at the portraits and reading the card, her entire demeanor changed. She bounced out of her chair, handed the card to me and commissioned my brothers to hang the paintings facing each other over the fireplace. She stepped back and looked for a long while. With sparkling, tear-filled eyes and a wide smile, she quickly turned and said, "I knew Daddy would be with us on Christmas Day!"

I glanced at the gift card scrawled in my father's handwriting. "Mother—Our daughter reminded me why I am so blessed. I'll be looking at you always—Daddy."

Sarah A. Rivers

A Gift of Faith

Growing up in suburban Baltimore, my brother, sister and I were typical kids. What set us apart from the other children in the neighborhood was our Irish Catholic upbringing. We were the "Catholic-school" kids. All of our friends went to the public school. They got to ride the school bus. They got new clothes every fall. They always talked about people we only knew from their yearbooks. And they definitely weren't forced to go to Mass every Saturday night!

Some of my friends went to church with their families. I even went with them a few times, but I often found myself defending my Catholic beliefs. Many times I'd come home and ask my mother questions like *why* we prayed to the Blessed Mother.

My younger brother, Chris, questioned our religion for different reasons. A sensitive kid, he was always disturbed by news reports of violence and famine. As a result, the question he would often ask my mother is, "How do you know there is a God?"

My mother enjoyed these conversations. She would sit for hours in her rocking chair, happy to share her beliefs, and hoping to provide comfort and strength to her children as they grew into independent young adults. Her faith was always evident. She lived her life the way she thought God wanted her to. That is one reason why she was okay with the thought of dying. She often said, "When it's my time, it's my time. It's not up to me." She accepted God's will for what it was.

Her faith sustained her through every challenge in life. It wasn't until the Persian Gulf War that I realized how powerful that faith could be. Fresh out of college and a young army officer, I had no idea what a war would be like. When I got deployed to Saudi Arabia, my mother sent me a card that read, "God grant me the serenity to accept the things I cannot change, the courage to change the things I can and the wisdom to know the difference." I kept that card next to my pillow so it would be the last thing I'd see at night and the first thing I'd see in the morning.

After I had my own children, I started to realize how special the relationship between a mother and her children is. I had always loved my mother, but once I became one, I began to really appreciate her. When I was younger, I had sworn I'd do something more than "just" be a mom, which seemed so trivial, so unimportant. As events unfolded, however, I found myself making sacrifices for my family. I learned how powerful a mother truly is.

My mother and I talked about that when my three girls were little. We talked about everything. She really was my best friend. We'd end our conversations with her saying, "Mother loves you." I'd answer it with, "Daughter loves you." She knew how I felt because she had lost her own mother shortly after my older sister, Kathy, was born. It made my mom sad that she never told her mother how much she appreciated her. Ironically, I never fully understood the depth of the pain she felt after her mother died until she herself passed away in May 1997.

I was living in Indiana at the time, thirty-one years old

and pregnant with my fourth child. I was looking forward to having the baby because I knew my mother would come and cook for me. I even told that to my husband the Thursday night before Memorial Day weekend, after a long day of morning sickness and taking care of my three small girls. As soon as I said it, the phone rang.

My brother-in-law was calling to tell me my mother was in the intensive care unit. Her heart had stopped as she was working out that afternoon at the health club. At fifty-seven, she was in pretty good shape. She and my father enjoyed an active social life and, though she had been on heart medication for years, she never let it slow her down.

Fortunately, a doctor, an off-duty firefighter and a nurse happened to be working out at the club and were able to revive her with CPR. She had no recollection of her ordeal and seemed fine to everyone who spent the weekend visiting her in the hospital. On Monday, they moved her to a private room with a phone, giving me an opportunity to talk with her. I teased her because she didn't remember seeing any white lights at the end of the tunnel. She assured me that if she had to go, that was the way she wanted to do it because she didn't feel anything, and it happened quickly.

"At least hold off till this baby is born," I remember saying to her, half-joking, half-serious.

Her response: "When it's my time, it's my time. I'm ready if the Lord wants me."

"That's great for you," I said, "but none of us are ready for you to go yet."

What she said next were the last words I remember her saying to me. They were the beautiful culmination of thirty-one years of my Irish Catholic upbringing all summed up in a humorous, heartfelt flubbing of the lines: "May the road rise up to meet you, may the wind be always at your back, and may God hold you in the palm of his hands, until we meet again." We said good-bye, hung up, and I knew I'd never talk to her again. *Daughter loves you*, I thought.

She was scheduled for an operation on Tuesday morning. If all went well, she'd be released on Wednesday. Unfortunately, my father got a call around six in the morning on Tuesday. Her heart had stopped again. He and Chris rushed to the hospital and were led to a waiting room. They waited until a nurse named Bobbie came out and said to my brother, "Are you Chris?"

Days later I called Bobbie to hear her tell the story. My mother's heart had stopped, and the hospital staff had rushed in to revive her. She had been gone for about forty-five minutes. "We didn't want to stop. She was too young," Bobbie told me. Certainly, all hope was lost; still, they had persisted. Suddenly, my mother's eyes opened! She reached up and grabbed Bobbie's arm, looked into her eyes and said with great urgency, "There is a God! I saw his face! Tell Chris, there is a God!" And then, my mother was gone.

Our mother, who constantly reaffirmed our faith in life, did so even more in death. When I heard the story, I remembered the many times I'd seen my mother praying the Rosary, sometimes even using her fingers to count the Hail Mary's. So many times she had asked for the Blessed Mother's intercession, "Holy Mary, Mother of God, pray for us sinners, now and at the hour of our death." Her prayers were answered. Mary's gift to our mother was our mother's gift to us—the gift of faith. There is a God.

Kelly E. Kyburz

I'll Make You a Rainbow

Looking back, I've often thought the doctors should have written a death certificate for me as well as my son, for when he died, a part of me died, too.

Andy was almost twelve. For over three years he had been battling cancer. He'd gone through radiation and chemotherapy; he'd gone into remission and come out again, not once but several times. I was amazed at his resiliency; he just kept getting up each time the cancer knocked him flat. Perhaps it was his pluckiness and grit that shaped my own attitude about Andy's future, or maybe I was simply afraid to face the possibility of his death. Whatever the cause, I always thought Andy would make it. He would be the kid who beat the odds.

For three summers, Andy had gone to a camp for kids with cancer. He loved it and seemed to relish the week he could forget about hospitals and sickness and just be a kid again. The day after he returned from his third camp adventure, we went to the clinic for a routine checkup. The news was bad. The doctor scheduled a bone-marrow transplant two days later in a hospital three hundred miles from our home. The next day we threw our things in a suitcase and left.

One of the things I tossed into my suitcase was the present Andy had brought me from camp—a plastic sun catcher shaped like a rainbow with a suction cup to attach it to a window. Like most mothers, I considered any present from my child a treasure and wanted it with me.

We arrived at the hospital and began the grueling ordeal the doctors said was my son's only chance. We spent seven weeks there. They turned out to be the last seven weeks of Andy's life.

We never talked about dying—except once. Andy was worn out and must have known he was losing ground. He tried to clue me in. Nauseous and weak after one of the many difficult procedures he regularly endured, he turned to me and asked, "Does it hurt to die?"

I was shocked, but answered truthfully, "I don't know. But I don't want to talk about death, because you are not going to die, Andy."

He took my hand and said, "Not yet, but I'm getting very tired."

I knew what he was telling me, but I tried hard to ignore it and keep the awful thought from entering my mind.

I spent a lot of my days watching Andy sleep. Sometimes I went to the gift shop to buy cards and notepaper. I had very little money, barely enough to survive. The nurses knew our situation and turned a blind eye when I slept in Andy's room and ate the extra food we ordered off of Andy's tray. But I always managed to scrape a bit together for the paper and cards because Andy loved getting mail so much.

The bone-marrow transplant was a terrible ordeal. Andy couldn't have any visitors because his immune system was so compromised. I could tell that he felt more isolated than ever. Determined to do something to make it easier for him, I began approaching total strangers in the waiting rooms and asking them, "Would you write my son a card?" I'd explain his situation and offer them a card or some paper to write on. With surprised expressions on their faces, they did it. No one refused me. They took one look at me and saw a mother in pain.

It amazed me that these kind people, who were dealing with their own worries, made the time to write Andy. Some would just sign a card with a little get-well message. Others wrote real letters: "Hi, I'm from Idaho visiting my grandmother here in the hospital..." and they'd fill a page or two with their story, sometimes inviting Andy to visit their homes when he was better. Once a woman flagged me down and said, "You asked me to write your son a couple of weeks ago. Can I write him again?" I mailed all these letters to Andy and watched happily as he read them. Andy had a steady stream of mail right up until the day he died.

One day, I went to the gift store to buy more cards and saw a rainbow prism for sale. Remembering the rainbow sun catcher Andy had given me, I felt I had to buy it for him. It was a lot of money to spend, but I handed over the cash and hurried back to Andy's room to show him.

He was lying in his bed, too weak to even raise his head. The blinds were almost shut, but a crack of sunlight slanted across the bed. I put the prism in his hand and said, "Andy, make me a rainbow." But Andy couldn't. He tried to hold his arm up, but it was too much for him.

He turned his face to me and said, "Mom, as soon as I'm better, I'll make you a rainbow you'll never forget."

That was one of the last things Andy said to me. Just a few hours later, he went to sleep and during the night, slipped into a coma. I stayed with him in the intensive care unit, massaging him, talking to him and reading him his mail, but he never stirred. The only sound was the constant drone and beepings of the life-support machines surrounding his bed. I was looking death straight in the face, but still I thought there'd be a last-minute save, a miracle that would bring my son back to me.

After five days, the doctors told me his brain had stopped functioning, and it was time to disconnect him from the machines keeping his body alive.

I asked if I could hold him. Just after dawn, they brought a rocking chair into the room, and after I settled myself in the chair, they turned off the machines and lifted him from the bed to place him in my arms. As they raised him from the bed, his leg made an involuntary movement, and he knocked a clear plastic pitcher from his bedside table onto the bed.

"Open the blinds," I cried. "I want this room to be full of sunlight!" The nurse hurried to the window to pull the cord.

As she did so, I noticed a sun catcher in the shape of the rainbow attached to the window, left no doubt by a previous occupant of this room. I caught my breath in wonder. Then, as the light filled the room, it hit the pitcher lying on its side on the bed, and everyone stopped what they were doing in silent awe.

The room was filled with flashes of color, dozens and dozens of rainbows on the walls, the floors, the ceiling, on the blanket wrapped around Andy as he lay in my arms— the room was alive with rainbows.

No one could speak. I looked down at my son, and he had stopped breathing. Andy was gone, but even in the shock of that first wave of grief, I felt comforted. Andy had made the rainbow that he promised me—the one I would never forget.

Linda Bremner

Seven White, Four Red, Two Blue

One joy shatters a hundred griefs.

Chinese Proverb

I believe every object in our lives holds a memory. The most prized object in my life, and the one that holds the most memories, is a rusty tin box. I need only look at the beat-up old tin box, resting obscurely on my bookshelf next to a picture of my five-year-old daughter, to unleash a flood of memories and emotions. Some happy—some sad—all mine.

The first true love of my life, and the one that still causes the most pain, was a Japanese girl named Hitomi. In Japanese her name meant Pure Beauty, but you didn't need to speak the language to understand that. You just had to look at her. I was twenty-six and she was twenty-one when we first met at a nightclub in Okinawa, Japan. I swear she came straight out of a fairy tale. She had long, straight, silky black hair that flowed to her perfectly shaped waist and highlighted her hundred-and-five-pound frame. Her skin was soft and tanned and seemed to glow in the sunlight; but what I remember most were her eyes. Her eyes seemed to pass right through me and touch the very depth of my soul. I was in love.

We started dating shortly after that first meeting. Hitomi was a very sentimental person. Every day held special importance to her. I would soon understand why.

One day, after we had been going out for about a month, she showed up at my apartment and handed me something. "Present," she said. I opened the carefully wrapped handkerchiefs she had used as gift wrap. What I saw surprised me—a beat-up, old, rusted, lime green, tin cigar box. The lid had the remains of a picture on the outside. Through the rust and chipped paint I could only make out what appeared to be a finger and an ear. The rest of the box looked just as bad—like it had been dragged behind a car after a wedding sixty years ago.

"Thanks," I told her. "If we're exchanging junk, let me get something out of my garbage for you."

She didn't understand my attempt at humor. "Open," she said, picking up the box and handing it to me. Paint and rust fell from it as I gripped the box in my hands. I was reluctant to open it, fearing it might still contain the remains of the world's first fruitcake. "Open," she said again, this time smacking me on the side of my head and pushing the box into my chest. I opened the box and was amazed. The inside was finished in gold leaf, polished and shined like a mirror.

In the box was a single, white, origami paper swan. "Every month we are together I will make you a white swan to put in our box," she said. "After one year, we will string the swans together to hang on the praying tree in front of Nishiohama Temple. This will be our way of thanking God for our time together. I will make you a blue swan to put in the box to show our one year of love together. And if we ever have an argument or fight, I will make us a red swan, so when we see it in our box we will remember what we did wrong and learn from it as a couple." We placed two strings of white swans on the tree at the temple while we were together. And in time, a few red ones appeared in our box as well.

It was during the middle of our third year together that Hitomi began to get sick. She had told me she had health problems in the past, but they were nothing for me to worry about. That was the only lie Hitomi ever told me. I found out through her best friend that she had leukemia and was in the final stages of that sickening disease. Her parents admitted her to the hospital, and after several weeks of pleading, they finally let me see her. I sat next to her bed and softly kissed her lips. When she saw me she smiled.

"Hello, honey," she whispered. Then she pointed to the nightstand next to her bed. "Please open for me." I opened the nightstand and saw within it a single, white paper swan. "I want to take to your house but too sick. I'm sorry. Now you please put in our box, okay?"

I nodded and kissed her forehead—tears flowing down my cheeks. I didn't notice how frail she had become. Or that her skin, once tanned and glowing, was now pale and gray. I also didn't notice that the long, silky hair she meticulously combed every day was gone, due to heavy doses of chemotherapy. I didn't see any of that. To me she was as beautiful as the first day we met, maybe even more so. It was then that I realized I wasn't looking at her—I was looking inside her. I saw the beauty in her that could never be changed. I saw what was important. I now understood the meaning of that tin box she gave me. It was her way of preparing me for what she knew would inevitably become of her—her way of teaching me that pure beauty is on the inside. And that no matter how broken or old the outside may appear, what's important—

what's real—is that which is held inside.

Hitomi died two days later. Her family didn't allow me at her funeral. I was a foreigner. That was fine. I knew she was with me, and she always would be—every time I opened that old tin box.

I once read, "No one knows what any object means except he or she who owns it." When I look at that tin box I think how true that is. Since her death, people have asked me about the relationship I had with Hitomi. My answer is as perplexing to them as it is simple to me: "Seven white, four red and two blue."

Robert P. Curry

Joseph's Living Legacy

In helping others, we shall help ourselves, for whatever good we give out completes the circle and comes back to us.

Flora Edwards

With loving tenderness I unpacked my son Joseph's Little League trophy, his stack of X-Man comics and the framed pictures of elephants that had decorated his bedroom walls back in our old apartment. Just two weeks before, Joseph had so looked forward to moving into his own room in the new house. Now, making his bed, I couldn't hold back the tears. *My little boy will never sleep here,* I grieved. *I'll never glimpse his smile again or feel his loving hug.*

Wondering how I could possibly manage to go on, I began unpacking the dozens of plush animals Joseph loved to collect—bears and monkeys, chipmunks and giraffes.

Sitting on his bed, I hugged the Chris Columbus bear he used to nuzzle when he was little and I read *Love You Forever* or another of his favorite stories. Joseph loved books, and to him they were especially precious because he had a learning disability that made it all but impossible for him to read them himself.

But Joseph was a determined little boy who refused to let his disability stop him from learning. He listened to his schoolbooks and tests on tape, and every night we sat together at the kitchen table so I could read his math problems to him and help him with his spelling. Joseph worked so hard; he always made honor roll at school. He also earned a green belt in karate and was pitcher for his Little League baseball team.

In many ways Joseph was just a regular little boy who loved playing video games with his brother, David, or going to the movies with his sister, Shalom. But Joseph also knew what it was like to feel different and need a helping hand.

I can't remember how many times I spotted Joseph carrying groceries for one of our elderly neighbors or refusing money after shoveling their cars out from the snow. He loved putting on puppet shows for the little girl down the street with Down's syndrome, and once, when doctors thought his friend Micah might need a kidney transplant, my son came to me and said, "I sure wish I could give him one of mine."

Joseph, my little *mensch*, always made me proud, even on the last day of his life.

I was folding clothes in the den that Saturday afternoon when out of nowhere my husband, Lou, shouted for me to call 911. He and Joseph had been discussing a movie they planned to see when suddenly Joseph collapsed onto his bed complaining of a terrific headache. His breathing grew ragged, and then it stopped. Lou, who is a physician, performed artificial respiration until the paramedics arrived. Then he called ahead to the ER while I rode in the ambulance with Joseph and prayed he wouldn't die.

Joseph, always the picture of health, had suffered a

massive brain aneurysm. "Is he going to die?" I asked my husband. Holding me tightly he answered, "Yes."

It seemed impossible. Only an hour ago my son was home watching TV—and now he was on life support with no hope of ever regaining consciousness. I wanted to cry out in shock and grief.

But there wasn't time. There was something important I had to do—and I had to do it right away.

"We have to donate his organs," I told Lou, recalling the time Joseph wanted to give a kidney to Micah. "It's what he would have wanted us to do."

A transplant coordinator made all the arrangements, and a few hours later our family gathered at Joseph's bedside to offer a prayer and say our last good-byes.

Then we went home, and throughout that night while surgeons recovered my son's organs I lay curled on his bed, clutching his favorite blanket and telling him how much I would always love him.

I don't know how I survived those next two weeks—the funeral and moving into the house we'd already contracted to buy. I cried every time I went near Joseph's new bedroom—the one he would have loved, if only he'd lived. There was a gaping hole in my heart.

Then one day when I felt I could bear my grief no longer, a letter came from the transplant coordinator. "I am writing to share the outcome of your generosity," I read with tears spilling down my cheeks.

Two Kentucky women, one of them the mother of a boy Joseph's age, were now off dialysis because they had each received one of my son's kidneys. Meanwhile, in Missouri, cells from Joseph's liver were helping to keep a critically ill transplant candidate alive while doctors waited for a matching donor organ to become available. In California two young children would soon be able to run and play with the healthy new heart valves my son had bequeathed them. And two teenagers, one from Kentucky and the other from New York, had regained their eyesight thanks to Joseph's corneas.

Seven people's lives had been changed dramatically because of my son. I carried the letter with me for days, reading and rereading it and marveling especially at the teens who'd received Joseph's corneas. Joseph's learning disability had prevented him from reading. But because of his very special gift there were now two more children in the world who could. Somehow, this helped me under-stand that my son had not lost his life in vain.

I wanted each and every one of Joseph's recipients to know who he was. So one night I wrote them each a letter and told them all about the little boy who had given them the ultimate gift. I asked the transplant agency to forward the letters to all seven recipients. With each I sent along one of his beloved stuffed animals and a copy of a school essay that he'd once written describing how to take care of them.

Knowing the good my son had brought into the world made it easier to walk past his room without bursting into tears. It helped the rest of the family, too, and eventually we became able to share happy memories of Joseph around the dinner table and at other family gatherings.

Lou and I also honored Joseph's memory by speaking to community groups and high-school students about the importance of organ donation. After a TV interview, the mother who had received one of Joseph's kidneys con-tacted us.

"I don't know how to thank you," she sobbed the day we first met.

"Seeing a part of my son living on is thanks enough for me," I said. Because of her new kidney, the woman had been able to attend her own son's eighth-grade gradua-tion. Joseph never reached the eighth grade, but instead of begrudging the woman her happiness, I *kvelled* in it—because it was my son who had made this miracle possible.

My son is gone, but in a very real way he still lives on, doing what he always did best—offering a helping hand to others in need. Some say Joseph's life was brief. I say it was full.

I once heard that if you save a life, you save the world. Well, my son saved five lives and gave the gift of sight to two others. What mother could possibly ask any more of her child? What mother could possibly be any prouder?

Kathie Kroot
As told to Heather Black

To Remember Me

The day will come when my body will lie upon a white sheet neatly tucked under four corners of a mattress located in a hospital busily occupied with the living and the dying. At a certain moment a doctor will determine that my brain has ceased to function and that, for all intents and purposes, my life has stopped.

When that happens, do not attempt to instill artificial life into my body by the use of a machine. And don't call this my deathbed. Let it be called the Bed of Life, and let my body be taken from it to help others lead fuller lives.

Give my sight to the man who has never seen a sunrise, a baby's face or love in the eyes of a woman. Give my heart to a person whose own heart has caused nothing but endless days of pain. Give my blood to the teenager who was pulled from the wreckage of his car, so that he might live to see his grandchildren play. Give my kidneys to one who depends on a machine to exist from week to week. Take my bones, every muscle, every fiber and nerve in my body and find a way to make a crippled child walk.

Explore every corner of my brain. Take my cells, if

necessary, and let them grow so that someday, a speech-less boy will shout at the crack of a bat and a deaf girl will hear the sound of rain against her window.

Burn what is left of me and scatter the ashes to the winds to help the flowers grow.

If you must bury something, let it be my faults, my weaknesses and all prejudice against my fellow man.

Give my sins to the devil. Give my soul to God.

If, by chance, you wish to remember me, do it with a kind deed or word to someone who needs you. If you do all I have asked, I will live forever.

Robert N. Test

The Pencil Box

I was deep in thought at my office preparing a lecture to be given that evening at a college across town when the phone rang. A woman I had never met said she was the mother of a seven-year-old boy and that she was dying. She said her therapist had advised her that discussing her pending death with her little boy would be too traumatic for him, but somehow that didn't feel right to her.

Knowing that I worked with grieving children, she asked my advice. I told her that our heart is often smarter than our brain, and that I thought she knew what would be best for her son. I also invited her to attend the lecture that night since I was speaking about how children cope with death. She said she would be there.

I wondered later if I would recognize her at the lecture, but my question was answered when I saw a frail woman being half-carried into the room by two adults. I talked about the fact that children usually sense the truth long before they are told, and they often wait until they feel adults are ready to talk about it before sharing their concerns and questions. I said that children usually can handle truth better than denial, even though the denial is intended to protect them from pain. I said that respecting children meant including them in the family sadness, not shutting them out.

At the break, she hobbled to me and said through her tears, "I knew it in my heart. I just knew I should tell him." She said that she would that night.

The next morning I received another phone call from her. I managed to hear the story through her choked voice. She said she awakened him when they got home the night before and quietly said, "Derek, I have something to tell you."

He quickly interrupted her, saying, "Oh, Mommy, is it now that you are going to tell me that you are dying?"

She held him close, and they both sobbed while she said, "Yes."

After a few minutes the little boy wanted down. He said he had something for her that he had been saving. In the back of one of his drawers was a dirty pencil box. Inside the box was a letter written in simple scrawl. It said, "Good-bye, Mom. I will always love you."

How long he had been waiting to hear the truth, I don't know. I do know that two days later Mom died. In her casket was placed a dirty pencil box and a letter.

Doris Sanford

2

THE POWER OF SUPPORT

Friendship improves happiness and abates misery, by the doubling of our joy and the dividing of our grief.

Albert Camus

When No Words Seem Appropriate

Many things, beyond a doubt, remain to be said which others will say with greater force and brilliance. But we need have no hope that one will utter on this Earth the word that shall put an end to our uncertainties. It is very probably, on the contrary, that no one in this world, nor perhaps in the next, will discover the great secret of the universe. Behold us then before the mystery of the cosmic consciousness.

Maurice Maeterlinck

I won't say "I know how you feel"—because I don't. I've lost parents, grandparents, aunts, uncles and friends, but I've never lost a child. So how can I say I know how you feel?

I won't say "You'll get over it"—because you won't. Life will have to go on. The washing, cooking, cleaning, the common routine. These chores will take your mind off your loved one, but the hurt will still be there.

I won't say "Your other children will be a comfort to you"—because they may not be. Many mothers I've talked to say that after they have lost a child, they easily lose their temper with their remaining children. Some even feel resentful that they're alive and healthy when the other child is not.

I won't say "Never mind, you're young enough to have another baby"—because that won't help. A new baby will fill your hours, keep you busy and give you sleepless nights. But it will not replace the one you've lost.

You may hear all these platitudes from your friends and relatives. They think they are helping. They don't know what else to say. Many will avoid you because they can't face you. Others will talk about the weather, the holidays and the school concert but never about how you're coping.

So what will I say?

I will say "I'm here. I care. Anytime. Anywhere." I will talk about your loved one. We'll laugh about the good memories. I won't mind how long you grieve. I won't tell you to pull yourself together.

No, I don't know how you feel—but with sharing, perhaps I will learn a little of what you are going through. And perhaps you'll feel comfortable with me and find your burden has eased. Try me.

Written by a Pediatric Nurse to Ann Landers

What You Can Do for a Grieving Friend

The most precious moments in friendship were not when I laughed with a friend, though those times are so good, but when I cried with a friend and she reached out and listened and understood.

Fran Morgan

The husband of my best friend called me from the hospital. As soon as I heard his voice, I knew the worst: Their lovely nineteen-year-old, Hilary, was going to die. "It's spread," he said, sounding rough and angry. "They're going to try some experimental drug, but they don't hold out much hope. Molly's with her now."

"Oh, David . . . David . . ." I whispered, searching for the words. What does one say at such a moment? What phrases could possibly be a match for the enormity of the plain and awful facts?

None. A man whose son was killed by a drunk driver had taught me that. He said, "I hated people saying, 'I know how you feel' or 'I share your pain.' How could they know the misery as sharp as a thousand splinters of glass inside me? How could they be sharing that?"

"What *could* they say?" I asked.

He thought a minute before answering. "All I wanted them to say was, 'I'm sorry.' It was the only thing that meant anything to me, just a simple 'I'm sorry.'"

Remembering his words, I said, "David, I'm so sorry. I'm so very sorry."

And later that night, when I met Molly at their front door and we clung to each other, I said, "I'm so dreadfully sorry." After a while I told her, "I've made fresh coffee. It's on the stove. I'll be back about nine in the morning."

That's something else I've learned. I try not to ask, "What can I do?" Instead, I think of something that may be welcome like fresh coffee, then go ahead and do it. "The best thing a friend did when my mother died," said a teacher, "was to call and say, 'I'm bringing dinner tomorrow night. If you don't need it, just put it in the freezer.'"

People in crisis may be in shock. They can scarcely hear the well-meant "What can I do?" let alone summon up a vision of what needs to be attended to. Thus, the biggest help may be to make a specific offer such as "I'll walk the dog, shall I?" or "I'll stay here to answer the phone if you like." The suggestion allows the person not to have to think if it seems beyond her at the moment, and the question allows her to say no if what you're offering is an intrusion.

Molly could have said no to my coming at nine in the morning, but she didn't. I thought she might want to talk, but she barely looked up when I came in. She was on her hands and knees scrubbing the kitchen floor. Only when I noticed she was polishing the same spot over and over did I realize she was scrubbing to keep from going to pieces.

When there was nothing more to clean, I said, "Come on, Molly, we're going for a walk." I didn't ask if she wanted to; how could Molly be asked to want anything but her daughter well and alive? I got her coat, held it as she put it on and took her arm.

We walked through the pine woods in the back of her house, our footsteps so muffled by the needled path that a doe and her fawn didn't take alarm until we were almost upon them. When we came out at the shore of the pond where our families often picnicked, we stood staring out across the winter water. Dark and still, it was not the friendly pond of summer but cold and bottomless.

"I wonder if death is like that," Molly finally said.

I longed to cry out, *No, no, it must be kinder.* But I echoed, "I wonder."

She said, not really to me, "How am I going to get through the next weeks?"

I forced myself not to be reassuring. "I don't know, Molly," I answered quietly. "I just don't know."

Months later, she told me that was the moment she knew she would find a way. It's hard to describe, but I knew what she meant because once it had happened to me. People said kind, well-meaning things like "You have to be brave" and "You'll get over this." But all I thought was, *You're not me. You don't understand.* Then someone said, "It's going to be very, very, hard; you've got a long way to go," and suddenly I knew I was going to make it. Someone had listened to me, had heard my despair, and instead of trying to talk me out of it, had accepted it.

To listen, to be there, to accept—that is the emotional first aid we can offer each other when a bad time comes.

Molly asked whether I thought she and David should be honest with Hilary or try to pretend her illness wasn't serious. In talking it over, I described a former neighbor, a much older woman, whose husband lay in bed with stomach cancer. She often came into my kitchen and slumped down exhausted, needing a few minutes' rest from the effort of keeping a cheerful face. Even when her husband said, "Look, Reb, you and I both know what this is," she couldn't give up the game. "No, no," she insisted, "you're going to be all right."

Do people want to be spared the knowledge they are dying? If you listen carefully, the dying person himself will often let you know. Doctors say they hear it in how a question is phrased. If a patient says, "I don't have cancer, do I?" it is likely that he does not want to know. But if he says, "I have cancer, don't I?" then he may be ready to talk about it.

Dying is a lonely business if you can't share your feelings. Physicians at the University of California Medical Center found that, of a group of children with leukemia, the ones whose parents denied the seriousness of their condition were the loneliest because they had no one to talk to about their fears.

This is not to say that family or friends should be aggressively frank and insist on the truth even if the patient doesn't want to hear it. That happens sometimes, I think, when people want to prove they can talk fearlessly of dying and death. But you should not be brave on someone else's time. Let them tell you what they want to know.

That's what Molly decided to do with Hilary. As it turned out, though, the doctor had been in to visit Hilary and she had asked him. Not *what* she had—she had already sensed that—but how long. He had told her weeks. She was dressed when Molly got there. "Please, Mom," she said, "take me home. That's all I really want now—to be home with you and Dad."

One evening after supper, Molly finished the dishes and went quietly down the hall. The only light in the living room was firelight. Hilary and her father, almost hidden in easy chairs, were talking—sometimes as father and daughter, sometimes as two people trying to find their way in a sea of mystery.

Quite easily and naturally, David was able to ask Hilary, "If this new drug doesn't work as we hope, is there anything you want us to know?"

"That I love you and Mom, always," said Hilary softly, "even when I acted like I didn't. That I'd like to be buried in that little country cemetery we found that day we were driving in through the valley. And that I hope you won't throw my diaries away. I'd like you to put them as far back under the eaves in the attic as possible—and to leave them there even if you move. Then maybe someday somebody will find them there and read them, and it won't be like I never lived."

"Imagine what we would have missed," Molly said after Hilary was gone, "if we couldn't have talked of her dying. We wouldn't have known her wishes. We could have missed what, in a funny way, was the best part of our lives together because we were so extraordinarily close and open with each other those last days."

That closeness, that openness, can come about not just with families, but also with friends. Critic Leonard Probst wrote that his own life-threatening illness led people he had known only in the context of success to share with him "litanies of fear, failure, anxiety and frustration they had never spoken of." The point of visiting is not, of course, to dump your own burden of woe on the counterpane, any more than it is to match stories of sickness and suffering. But you can listen for cues. And if the person seems to want to explore deeper water and you are courageous enough to follow, it can be a time of intimacy and trust that is incomparable.

Even if all you talk about is everyday matters, however, your visit is still important. To convey love and warmth and respect is the most valuable kind of emotional support. Your presence alone does that, so don't let worries about what to say keep you away. The one gift only you can bring is yourself.

After a person has died, your thoughts turn to what you can do for the survivors. Again, the answer is much the same: Be there. Listen to them. Accept their grief.

I was struck by the grace and simplicity of Hilary's friends who came to the house the day after her death to say a few words and to hug Molly and David. They must have had thoughts like "Hilary's parents won't want to see anybody but family at a time like this" or "Other friends were closer than I was." But if they thought of such excuses, they had the sense to ignore them. They came because they cared—and just coming showed Molly and David they cared. "I'm sorry," they said. "I loved her, and I'm going to miss her." It was enough.

Hilary's tennis partner asked if he could have the small silver plate inscribed with her initials from the heel of her racquet; he wanted to put it on his own, he said, in her memory. A close friend asked for a string of azure beads Hilary often wore. And a neighborhood youngster said how kind Hilary had always been to her and could she please have Hilary's yellow T-shirt to hang in her room. I was a bit taken aback at these requests until I saw how it pleased Molly and David to know that Hilary's friends wanted to remember her.

A young man Hilary had gone out with a few times called from across the country to say how sorry he was. To my surprise, Molly started chuckling in the middle of the phone call, then laughed aloud. The young man was telling her a funny tale of a day he and Hilary went white-water rafting and tipped over. For a few moments Hilary, young and laughing and happy, was alive again.

How kind and unself-conscious it was of the young man to call. Did he stop to think that he wasn't a close friend? A friend of mine did, when she heard that some-one she knew only casually had lost both her parents within the same week. My friend reached for the telephone, stopped, then reached again, thinking, *Oh, well, she doesn't have to talk to me if I'm intruding.*

An hour later, they were still chatting, for the woman had been feeling terribly alone. The friendly, unexpected voice was a lifeline pulling her back to a warmer world. She still speaks of how grateful she was for the call.

Another friend had a similar experience on the receiving end. The morning the announcement of her mother's death appeared in the paper, a woman she hadn't seen since grammar school called. She spoke of butterscotch sundaes at Schrafft's, ice skating in the park, a matinee of *Pinocchio*—kindnesses the mother had included her in.

"Ever since then, I haven't hesitated to pick up the phone," my friend says. No one else called that morning— they didn't want to bother the family, I'm sure. But I can't tell you how consoling it was to know that somebody who hadn't seen my mother in years still remembered her with such fondness.

Curiously enough, our impulses in such circumstances are usually right. It's our second thoughts that trip us up. We have to learn to ignore that self-deprecating voice that says, *Oh, they won't want to hear from me,* or *I'll just be in the way,* or *Somebody else will call.*

Do call. Do go. Do reach out. Don't be put off by the thought that you won't know what to say. To bring emotional support to someone in crisis requires only this: Be loving. Be there.

Jo Coudert

Lot's Wife

Although the world is full of suffering, it is full also of overcoming it.

Helen Keller

Enid was an older woman whose husband had died unexpectedly two years before she came to see me. Withdrawn and distant, she had not cried or spoken of his death to anyone in all that time. She no longer cooked or looked after her garden or her house. Most of the time she sat in her bathrobe in the living room, looking out the window at nothing at all. She had been given antidepressants by her doctor, but they had not made much difference, and after a while she had simply stopped taking them. "They won't bring him back," she had said. She had been brought to see me by one of her daughters who told me, "I lost both my parents the day my father died."

At first Enid and I sat and looked at each other in silence. She was a lovely woman in her early seventies, but she seemed as lifeless as the chair she sat on, as if she were only the wrapper that had once enclosed a life. She seemed so fragile that I wondered if she would have the strength to stay the full hour.

I opened the conversation by asking her why she had come. "My husband has died," she replied, turning her head away from me to look out my window. "My daughters would like me to talk about it, but I do not think that I care to." When I gently asked her to say more about this she said simply, "Talking seems a waste of time. No one could possibly understand."

I nodded in agreement. "Yes, of course," I said. "You have lost your life. Only your husband could understand what you have lost. Only he knew what your life together was like." At this she turned back to look at me. Her eyes were gray, like her hair. There was no light in them. I nodded again. "If he were here, Enid, what would you tell him?" I asked her.

She considered me for a long moment. Then she closed her eyes and began to speak to her husband aloud, telling him what life was like without him. She told him about going to their special places alone, walking their dogs alone, sleeping in their bed alone. She told him about needing to learn to do the little things he had always taken care of, things she had never known about. She reminded him of times that only he would remember, old memories that no one else had shared. And then for the first time since he died, she began to cry. She cried for a long time.

When her tears stopped, I asked her if there was anything she had not said. Hesitantly she told me how angry she was with him for abandoning her to grow old alone. She felt as if he had broken a promise to her. She missed him terribly and all that he had brought into her life.

"He was a teacher of love for me," she told me. The child of rigid and suspicious people, she had been amazed at her husband's selflessness, his readiness to extend his hand to others, even to strangers. She told me story after story of his generosity, his kindness, her eyes looking beyond me to the past. "Herbert always went the extra mile," she said. "So many people loved him."

I was deeply touched by Herbert and by the woman he had loved. "Enid," I asked her, "if Herbert were here, what would he say to you about the way you have lived the last two years of your life?" She looked startled. "Why, he would say, 'Enid, why have you built a monument of pain in memory of me? My whole life was about love.'" She paused. Then for the first time I saw the hint of a smile. "Perhaps there are other ways to remember him," she said.

Afterward she told me that she had felt that if she let go of her pain, she would betray Herbert's memory and diminish the value of his life. She now saw that she had indeed betrayed him by holding on to her pain and closing her heart. She never came back to see me again. Herbert had told her everything that she needed to hear.

Every great loss demands that we choose life again. We need to grieve in order to do this. The pain we have not grieved over will always stand between us and life. When we don't grieve, a part of us becomes caught in the past like Lot's wife who, because she looked back, was turned into a pillar of salt.

Grieving is not about forgetting. Grieving allows us to heal, to remember with love rather than pain. It is a sorting process. One by one you let go of the things that are gone, and you mourn for them. One by one you take hold of the things that have become a part of who you are and build again.

About a year after this meeting, Enid sent me a clipping from the local paper about a group of widows she had organized to help elderly people with the tasks they could not do for themselves in their homes. There was no note with the clipping, just a tiny one-breath poem she had written and signed. "Grief./ I pull up anchor,/ and catch the wind."

Rachel Naomi Remen, M.D.

THE FAMILY CIRCUS® **By Bil Keane**

"When a lady's husband dies,
why does she hafta be a window?"

Reprinted with permission from Bil Keane.

One So Young

The measure of life, after all, is not its duration but its donation.

Peter Marshall

Grieving over the death of my newborn twin sons taught me many lessons. The most important was, whatever the challenge, we all have enough strength within us, as long as we have enough support around us. I resolved to do my part in providing that support to as many grieving parents as possible, including gentle encouragement of the family to take advantage of every opportunity that would help them heal. Since the luxury of time for decision making is not allowed in the days following a death, time was of the essence. I never heard a grieving parent express regret for something they had done, but many times I'd heard, "I wish I had. . . ."

On a late winter evening, a mutual friend informed me that a young couple's baby had died the day before, apparently of sudden infant death syndrome (SIDS). She told me that the mother especially was having a very difficult time and asked if I would visit them.

Armed with photos of my own babies, I was met by the grieving father as I walked up the driveway.

"I'm so sorry," I said. He nodded and showed me into the house.

At the table, seemingly oblivious to my entrance, sat the baby's mom, Rhonda. She stared at her hands with swollen eyes. Our mutual friend and her daughter were with her, looking sad and feeling very helpless.

We were introduced, and Rhonda barely tipped her head in acknowledgment. I sat next to her and waited. When she offered no conversation, I started talking about my own experience with my twins. Although I was aware that in no way could I know what she was going through, I did want her to know that I had endured a similar situation, and yet I was still here, whole and alive.

Finally, Rhonda spoke about how she had found her daughter. Rhonda had picked the infant up and handed her to her husband, hoping beyond hope that Barry would be able to revive their baby. Automatically, he tried, but it soon became apparent that Sarah was dead.

When the coroner arrived, he placed baby Sarah on her parents' bed while he made his preliminary examination. Rhonda shivered, "How could I ever sleep there again?" Now it was clear. Not only did she detest death because it had separated her from her baby, but also because it had contaminated her home and family. Rhonda had little energy left, and she was spending the remainder on loathing her vile enemy.

I brought out the photos of my little boys. "When Josh and Cole died, we kept them with us for several hours," I said quietly.

For the first time, Rhonda looked at me, her eyes penetrating, searching my face for answers to questions she didn't even want to ask. I continued, "We took locks of hair, had our babies footprinted and just held them close."

"But they were dead!" Rhonda had stumbled into a territory so foreign to her that she couldn't even believe she was saying the words.

"Yeah. They were dead. But we had to make the transition from loving them as earthly bodies to loving them as spirits. It's one of the hardest things to learn to do, but it can be done. Even though the spark of who they were, their soul, was no longer in those little bodies, nonetheless, the bodies were there for us to hold. And for that, I will be eternally grateful."

She looked back at her hands. "Barry wants to go see her. He wants to say good-bye," she whispered. "I don't want to, though. . . ."

I knew that Rhonda was reliving all the feelings of horror that she felt when she found her still daughter. "She won't look the same as when you discovered her. She will be more peaceful," I offered.

After a good hour of mild persuasion, this young, frightened mother murmured, "Well, maybe I'll just take a peek. . . ."

Now I had to convince the staff at the small town hospital.

A phone call had me discussing the situation with an administrator, the head nurse and a social worker, until finally I was connected to the pathologist. I explained the scenario to a shocked and very reluctant doctor. "But I've already autopsied that baby!" he exclaimed.

"That's okay. It just means she has some stitches. We can deal with that."

"But I wouldn't want to see *my* kid that way!" He was incredulous.

I wanted to say that he wouldn't want to see his child dead either, but this family had to work around that reality.

Persistently, I told him about my own sons, and how we

had held them for hours. I could feel him starting to bend.

"Well, all right. But you have to come, too."

"Absolutely! I'll be there."

We parked our cars and as we walked toward the hospital entrance, I talked to Rhonda and Barry about the fact that men and women grieve differently. "After the initial phase, when you both support each other beautifully, men tend to not want to talk much about it. They want to get on with life and don't feel that they can do so when they think about their child constantly. So they put it aside. Now women, on the other hand, will talk to anyone who will listen, and sometimes even if they won't. They bring it all out, over and over, and heal from the inside out. The problem is, the mom thinks that the dad didn't really love the child since he doesn't seem to care. Whereas the dad thinks his partner has gone crazy because she is dwelling so much on it. The thing is, if you understand each other's method of grieving, you can get through it intact, as a couple. Just realize that Mom needs to get her support elsewhere for awhile, probably from another woman. But you must be aware that you both loved the baby just as much, and you both will miss her terribly." They walked in silence.

When we arrived at the room where Sarah was, we were met by the pathologist. He was obviously anxious, seemingly nervous that this young woman would pass out, or sue him, or maybe both. I left Rhonda and Barry in the hall. "I'll go in first."

I looked at the sweet baby in the bassinet. A bonnet covered the stitches on her head, and she was wrapped in a blanket. I noticed the area on her face where the blood had pooled after she died. I returned to the couple.

"She has some mottling on her cheek. It just looks like a bit of a bruise. And you'll notice that her lips look different—not as full. But that's all normal," I told them.

Rhonda reached inside herself and gathered every ounce of strength she could find. She marched into the room, like a soldier to war, the pathologist close behind. The attending nurse picked up little Sarah, and Rhonda immediately reached for and cuddled her daughter.

The doctor held his breath as Sarah's mom looked her over carefully and then glanced up at me, her eyes shining with emotion. "I told you she was beautiful, didn't I?" she beamed. The anger, fear and disgust visibly drained from the young mother. The transformation was miraculous, and the only adjective that could truly describe Rhonda now was peaceful.

I left her and Barry alone with their little girl and walked into the hall with the doctor. He nodded at me, smiled and returned to his duties. After a while Rhonda realized that Barry needed private time with Sarah, and she joined me, closing the door behind her.

As we left the hospital, a noticeably calmer Rhonda walked with us. She began to plan her baby's funeral, even including an open casket viewing. Later, when Barry lifted their eighteen-month-old son to see his little sister in the casket, Mathew pointed to her and declared, "Baby!"

And it was a serene, brave mom who stood at the front of the congregation and, with a steady voice, read a poem for her daughter.

Rhonda and Barry brought another baby girl into the world and named her Kathreen. She and her brother are much loved and appreciated in a way that only parents who have lost children can understand. Every moment, including the difficult ones, is experienced with gratitude, thankful for being able to nurture the gifts that are their children.

As is the way of the world, the events surrounding Sarah's death turned what could be viewed as a tragedy into an extraordinary formation of hope. Rhonda began facilitating grief support for bereaved parents, even accompanying some while seeing their dead babies. As she learned more about bereavement, she started to perceive a correlation between poverty and infant mortality. Eventually, her journey led her to work for a large antipoverty group in British Columbia.

Baby Sarah's impact on the world in which she lived so briefly is profound. Although I had never met her in life, she touched my heart in the way of an old, wise soul. The love that she brought to this Earth has grown with its own momentum, and it's spreading still, a gentle, healing wave, helping to wash away sorrow.

It's quite an accomplishment for one so young.

Diane C. Nicholson

Being There

Do you know of someone
Whose precious child has died?
Perhaps she is a neighbor or friend
With whom you can confide.
You assume that she is suffering
A tragedy so deep,
That there is nothing you can do
Since all she does is weep.
You feel that if you see her
There is nothing you can say
That would make her precious child come back
Or make the pain go away.
And if by chance you meet her
And have to face her grief,
You'll do your very best
To make this meeting brief.
You'll talk about the weather
Or the lady down the lane,
But you'll never mention her child—
That would cause her too much pain!
And when the funeral's over,
And all is said and done,

You'll go home to your family,
And she'll be all alone.
She'll go on, she'll be all right, time heals—
Or so it seems,
While she's left alone to pick up the pieces
Of her shattered life and dreams.

-OR-

You can open up your heart
And find that special place
Where compassion and true giving
Are awaiting your embrace.
"Today I'm thinking of you in a very special way,"
Or, how about "I love you!"
Are some loving things to say.
Sometimes a very simple task
Like picking up the phone,
Can help her feel not-so-quite
Desperately alone.
Whatever comes from a genuine heart
Cannot be said in vain
For the truth is, it's these very things
That lessen her great pain.
And when you let her talk about
Her child who is now dead,
You'll know this is far greater
Than anything you've said.
So will you reach out with all your soul
And let her know you care?
For in the end there's no substitute
For simply BEING THERE!

Debi L. Pettigrew

A New Strength

When someone dies, you don't get over it by forgetting; you get over it by remembering, and you are aware that no person is ever truly lost or gone once they have been in our life and loved us, as we have loved them.

Leslie Marmon Silko

"What's wrong, Mommy?" One by one, three small figures straggled into my bedroom, navigating through the darkness to my side of the bed. The ringing of the phone and my crying had pulled them from their sleep in the few minutes before sunrise.

"Mommy's very sad right now," their daddy answered for me. "Mommy's sad because your Grandpa Bastien died early this morning."

All three climbed onto the bed and started stroking me, each trying to comfort a pain I thought they were too young to understand. Three sets of innocent eyes stared helplessly up at me, watching unfamiliar waves of grief ebb and flow.

They did not know their grandpa the way I had hoped they would. A gap of seven hundred miles saw to that.

Their memories of Grandpa Bastien came from visits at Thanksgiving, long-distance phone calls and pictures displayed in photo albums. They did not know the big, strong man I knew and loved so much. And for once, I was glad their little hearts were spared knowing him so they would not feel the depth of losing him.

None of them had ever seen or heard me cry so openly. Through tears I reassured them I would be all right but there was no way to explain the grief. There was no way to tell a four-, six- and eight-year-old how their mommy's life had changed. In an instant I had gone from having a father to having memories. At that moment, thirty-four years of memories and pictures seemed small and insignificant.

It would have been selfish to give words to my tears, explain to them that I would never again hear his voice, send him Father's Day cards or hold his hand. No, I knew it would be wrong to make them understand this grief, so I held back the words and released only the tears. They continued their vigil, sitting quietly, patting me tenderly with little hands.

As the first hint of morning light filtered through the blinds in the bedroom, they began to talk softly amongst themselves. One by one they hugged me and kissed me. One by one they scooted off the bed and left the room.

Off to play or watch cartoons, I presumed, and I was glad grief had not touched their innocence.

I felt helpless, though, watching them walk away. With one phone call, I had crossed this ominous bridge between my father's life and his death, and I didn't know how to return. I didn't know how I would learn to laugh or play or be the mother they needed me to be in the midst of this grief. After lying in bed for what seemed like an eternity, I dried my eyes and decided I'd try to explain my sadness to them in a way they could understand. While still formulating the words, they walked back into the room, each with knowing eyes.

"Here, Mommy," they whispered in unison. "We made this for you."

I took the little package from eager hands and carefully peeled away a layer of leftover Christmas wrapping paper. Inside I found a note written by my eight-year-old: "To Mommy: We love you. Love, Shae, Andrew and Annie."

"Thank you," I told them. "This is beautiful."

"No, Mommy, turn it over," one of them instructed me.

I turned over the note and on the other side discovered a paper frame, decorated with crayon lines and hearts, and inside the frame was a photograph of my dad, smiling his contented smile, hands folded across an ample belly. It was one of the last good pictures I had taken before he died, before sickness had taken the sparkle from his eye.

My well-planned speech fell away, and I knew no explanation was needed. They understood my tears, and their handmade gift had given me new strength. As I looked at the picture, echoes of childhood memories flooded back, filling the emptiness. Yes, grief had touched my children, but they had their own special way of dealing with it. In their innocence, they taught me that the things I had thought insufficient, the memories and pictures, would be the very things to keep my dad alive.

Kara L. Dutchover

THE FAMILY CIRCUS® **By Bil Keane**

"My grandfather is in Florida."
"That's nothin'. Mine is in heaven."

The Wisdom of a Child

You're surprised when you find out that you're going to make it. . . . There is some kind of ability we all have that just shows up on your front porch.

Anonymous

Never had life been so difficult. As a veteran police officer, exposed to the constant stress and pressures inherent in the profession, the death of my life partner struck a hammer blow that pitched me into the depths of depression. At twenty-eight years of age, my beloved Liz had suffered a perforated colon as a complication of Crohn's disease and died tragically after several operations and six agonizing weeks in the intensive care unit. Our firstborn son, Seth, celebrated his fourth birthday the day following his mother's death, and Morgan, our youngest boy, would reach his third exactly three weeks later.

Liz, who had been a stay-at-home mother, excelled at cooking, housecleaning and all the other domestic chores that embellished our lives. In true macho-cop, chauvinistic fashion, I had taken her generosity for granted, never having time to take on any of these responsibilities myself. As a result I found myself suddenly, in the midst of my grief, thrust ranting and screaming into the role of maid, shopper, driver, launderer, childcare professional, cook and dishwasher. We had moved into a heavily mortgaged new home only weeks before Liz's death, and our financial situation was already precarious. I soon realized that police work, with its rotating shifts, would necessitate a live-in nanny, further taxing my already overburdened salary. To my great dismay, the constant demands for attention from two preschoolers left me exhausted and irritated, until I began to resent their very existence.

In the following days, loneliness and pain gave way to guilt, anger and, eventually, self-pity. I spiraled deeper and deeper into despair, and it wasn't long before my body began to display its inner turmoil. Despite my efforts to veil my grief from the children, my eyes became dark and baggy, my weight plummeted, and on one occasion, the boys watched me spill milk all over the table as a quivering hand thwarted my efforts to fill a glass.

Although I dreaded the moment, I knew at some point I would have to delve into the task of sorting through Liz's personal effects, cleaning out the closets and boxing up her clothes and other belongings. One evening, the boys tucked away for the night, I began. Each dress, that scarf, this pair of shoes, one by one, evoked its treasured, if not painful, memory and feelings of overwhelming guilt. It was in a small fold, deep within her purse, that I found almost by accident a neatly folded, tiny slip of yellowed paper, its creases, tight and crisp with age, protecting a carefully printed message.

"Dear Kevin," it began, "these are all the reasons that I love you . . ." and as I read on, her words obscured by tears, my heart ached and my body shook with convulsive, painful sobs of loneliness. I had hit bottom.

Slowly, in that hopeless fog of despair, I became aware of two small arms wrapped around my legs as I sat at the edge of the bed. A small voice asked in all the innocence of his three years, "What's the matter, Daddy?"

"I feel sad, Morgan, that Mommy's gone to heaven, and we won't see her for a very long time," I said, struggling vainly for composure.

"Don't worry, Daddy, we'll help you. When Seth and I get up in the morning, we'll put the cereal on the table and all you'll have to do is make the toast."

With those few, simple, loving words, my three-year-old child taught me a greater lesson than any other. His thoughts were sunlight filtering into the dreary, winter landscape of my soul, and I knew at that instant that life would be okay.

Kevin D. Catton

A Light in the Darkness

Shortly after our fifteen-year-old son, Adam, died, I wanted to do something as a public remembrance of him. I needed to let the outside world know that we were grieving thoroughly for the loss of all that Adam was and all that he would have been. I especially didn't want others to forget my son. Our house is nestled in a clearing in the woods and accessible only by a very long driveway. Passersby cannot see our house from the road. And so, on a blustery November day barely a month after he died, I tied a large white bow for our Adam on a tree by the side of the road at the end of our driveway. It was a sign of love, of hope, of sorrow beyond all comprehension. Throughout the past year, as the bow became tattered and worn, I replaced it several times and have even managed to grow a few white flowers at the base of the tree beneath that white bow. Little else that I have done for my son since he died has held as much significance to me as this white bow, which has come to symbolize Adam's life, death and our grief.

Just prior to leaving for a family gathering at my mother's house on a Christmas day, I was feeling, as I regularly do, that I wanted to do something special for Adam.

I made a luminaria with a gold angel on it; my husband, surviving son and I placed the luminaria under the white bow in the small flower garden. There, in the brilliance of a cold, clear Christmas afternoon, we lit a candle for our Adam. We added a second luminaria to burn in remembrance of all the children who have died. No one else could see the candles burning on that bright, sunlit day, but knowing they were there gave me a sense of peace. Last year, our first Christmas without Adam, the day had been unbearable; Adam's absence had been so pervasive. This year, all afternoon while I was at my mother's house, I thought of those luminarias burning by the side of the road for our Adam and all of the children who have died. I was uplifted and embraced by a sense of warmth I had not previously experienced.

It became apparent that those luminarias had also been of great importance to my husband and surviving son, for that evening, as we were preparing to leave my mother's house, we each wondered aloud if the candles would still be burning. Throughout the day, our thoughts of those luminarias had allowed each of us to endure the unendurable, and it now seemed crucial that the candles would still be lit when we returned home. My husband, surviving son and I NEEDED to see that very small flicker of light glowing through the darkness.

The ride home from my mother's house on Christmas night had always been a time of supreme bliss for me; my two boys tucked safely into the backseat of the car, each of us filled with the joy and wonder of the day. I had savored this time and counted my blessings. Last year, our first Christmas without Adam, I wept. But this year, I was focused on those candles and all they represented. We drove home in silence, each of us lost in our own private memories of Adam; each of us wishing that somehow, some way the candles still burned.

As we anxiously approached our driveway, we strained to distinguish a glimmer of light in the darkness of that Christmas night. And YES, the candles remained burning and so much brighter than we had expected! When we reached our driveway, our hearts soared as we saw that there, under the white bow in the very small flower garden by the side of the road, a third candle now burned with our two.

The third candle had been placed by two very caring people who undoubtedly understood the very profound nature of their very compassionate deed. They are bereaved parents as well, who on a cold, dark Christmas night had come to our home to secretly fill our mailbox with small, meaningful gifts. All to be discovered on another day, at another time. What they left behind was a promise of light, perhaps just a small flicker at first, but a light nonetheless, always burning through the darkness of our grief.

Nina A. Henry

3

COPING AND HEALING

I would say to those who mourn . . . look upon each day that comes as a challenge, as a test of courage. The pain will come in waves, some days worse than others, for no apparent reason. Accept the pain. Do not suppress it. Never attempt to hide grief.

Daphne du Maurier

Sorrow

In this sad world of ours, sorrow comes to all,
and it often comes with bitter agony.
Perfect relief is not possible,
except with time.
You cannot now believe that you will ever feel better.
But this is not true.
You are sure to be happy again.
Knowing this,
truly believing it,
will make you less miserable now.
I have had enough experience to make this statement.

Abraham Lincoln

Love and Water

Mama died just days before my eleventh birthday, and my destiny careened dramatically from snuggly to loose-ended. Overnight, my childhood vanished. In the coming months, Dad met Dot at work and began seeing her regularly. A year later, they married.

So much. So quickly. Another woman moving into our house stirred anew my still-fresh memories of Mama. At the same time, Dot inherited a brood of three children, ages five, eight and eleven.

When alone, I listened to an old recording of "You'll Never Walk Alone," and I was convinced my mama sang those words to me from the other side. Yet in moments of grief I wondered, *How can she walk with me now?* My child's heart yearned for a mother's touch.

"Do you want the kids to call you Mama?" Dad asked Dot one day. Something in me wanted her to say "yes."

Dot looked troubled for long moments, then said, "No. That wouldn't be right."

The *no* felt like a physical blow. *Blood's thicker'n water*, came my grandma's favorite litany. I'd not, until that very moment, grasped its meaning. My stepmother's answer seemed proof that blood *was* thicker, that I was merely

Daddy's "baggage"—proof that, to her—despite the fact that she introduced me as "my daughter"—I was biologically *not.*

I was of the *water.* So I distanced myself.

My sulky aloofness hid a deep, deep need for acceptance. Yet no matter how churlish I became, Dot never hurt me with harsh words. Ours was, in those trying days, a quiet, bewildered quest for harmony.

After all, we were stuck with each other. She had no more choice than I.

I visited Mama's grave every chance I got to talk things over with her. I never carried flowers because fresh arrangements always nestled lovingly against the headstone, put there, no doubt, by Daddy.

Then, in my fourteenth year, I came in from school one day and saw my newborn baby brother, Michael. I hovered over the bassinet, gently stroking the velvety skin as tiny fingers grasped mine and drew them to the little mouth. I dissolved into pure, maternal mush. Dot, still in her hospital housecoat, stood beside me.

In that moment, our gazes locked in wonder. "Can I hold him?"

She lifted and placed him in my arms.

In a heartbeat, that tiny bundle *snapped* us together.

"Like your new coat?" Dot asked that Christmas as I pulled the beautiful pimento-red topper from the gift package and tried it over my new wool sweater and skirt.

In a few short months, Dot had become my best friend.

At Grandma's house one Sunday, I overheard Dot tell my Aunt Annie Mary, "I told James I didn't think it was right to force the kids to call me Mama. Irene will always be Mama to them. That's only right." So that's why she'd said "no."

Or was it? *Blood's thicker'n water.* Was Grandma right? Was that always true in matters pertaining to familial loyalty? I shrugged uneasily, telling myself that it didn't matter anyway.

The following years, Dot embraced my husband Lee as "son," she soothed me through three childbirths, and afterward spent full weeks with me, caring and seeing to my family's needs. Intermittent with these events, she birthed three of her own, giving me two brothers and a sister. How special our children felt, growing up together, sharing unforgettable holidays like siblings.

In 1974, Lee and I lived two hundred miles away when a tragic accident claimed our eleven-year-old Angie. By nightfall, Dot was there, holding me. She was utterly heartbroken.

I moved bleakly through the funeral's aftermath, secretly wanting to die. Every Friday evening, I dully watched Dot's little VW pull into my driveway. "Daddy can't come. He has to work," she said. After leaving work, she drove four hours nonstop to be with me each weekend, a trek that continued for three long months.

During those visits, she walked with me to the cemetery, held my hand and wept with me. If I didn't feel like talking, she was quiet. If I talked, she listened. She was so *there* that, when I despaired, she single-handedly shouldered my anguish.

Soon, I waited at the door on Fridays. Slowly, life seeped into me again.

In 1992, Dad's sudden auto accident death yanked the earth from beneath me, and I lapsed into shock, inconsolable. My first reaction was that I needed Dot—my family.

Then, for the first time since adolescence, a cold, irrational fear blasted me with the force of TNT. Dad, my genetic link, *gone*. I'd grown so secure with the *Daddy and Dot* alliance through the years that I'd simply taken family solidarity for granted. Now with Dad's abrupt departure, the chasm he left loomed murky and frightening.

Had Dad, I wondered, *been the glue? Did glue equate genetic, after all?*

Terrifying thoughts spiraled through my mind as Lee drove me to join relatives. *Will I lose my family?* The peril of that jolted me to the core.

Blood's thicker'n water. If Grandma felt that way, couldn't Dot feel that way, too, just a little bit? The small child inside my adult body wailed and howled forlornly. It was in this frame of mind that I entered Dot's house after the accident.

Dot's house. Not Dad's and Dot's house anymore.

Will Daddy's void change her? She loved me, yes, but suddenly I felt keenly DNA-stripped, the stepchild of folklore. A sea of familiar faces filled the den. Yet, standing in the midst of them all, I felt utterly alone.

"Susie!" Dot's voice rang out, and through a blur I watched her sail like a porpoise to me. "I'm so sorry about Daddy, honey," she murmured and gathered me into her arms.

Terror scattered like startled ravens.

What she said next took my breath. She looked me in the eye and said gently, "He's with your Mama now."

I snuffled and gazed into her kind face. "He always put flowers on Mama's grave. . . ."

She looked puzzled, then smiled sadly. "No, honey, he didn't put the flowers on her grave."

"Then who . . . ?"

She looked uncomfortable for long moments. Then she leveled her gaze with mine. "I did."

"You?" I asked, astonished. "All those years?" She nodded, then wrapped me in her arms again.

Truth smacked me broadside. *Blood is part water.* Grandma just didn't get it.

With *love* blending them, you can't tell one from the other.

I asked Dot recently, "Isn't it time I started calling you Mom?"

She smiled and blushed. Then I thought I saw tears spring into her eyes.

"Know what I think?" I said, putting my arms around her. "I think Mama's looking down at us from heaven, rejoicing that you've taken such good care of us, doing all the things she'd have done if she'd been here. I think she's saying, 'Go ahead, Susie, call her Mom.'"

I hesitated, suddenly uncertain. "Is that okay?"

In a choked voice, she replied, "I would consider it an honor."

Mama's song to me was true: I do not walk alone.

Mom walks with me.

Emily Sue Harvey

Garrit

My son Garrit died eighteen months ago. We were on safari in Botswana when a spotted hyena took him from his tent just after midnight, dragged him into the bush and killed him. Eleven years old, he died quickly, but his small body was left mutilated and torn apart.

Only hours before his death, he listened to me read to him while he lay burrowed beneath his blankets. When I'd kissed him good night, he thanked me for bringing him to Botswana, then said, "I can't wait until tomorrow." Had he not been killed that night, we'd have spent the next day viewing pods of hippos, animals that never failed to bring a smile to Garrit's lips. Garrit was more precious to me than anyone or anything I've ever known. His last words, "I can't wait until tomorrow," are etched in my mind just as the smell and feel of my son will always remain a part of me. At the same time, Garrit's death transformed my world into a no-man's-land, a place marked by shock and disbelief, a barren landscape stripped bare of life—unrecognizable, incomprehensible. I felt as if I, too, had been torn apart inside.

For we don't expect our children to die. It doesn't fit within the natural order of things. Don't we instinctively protect them from illness and danger from the moment they are born? Aren't they supposed to outlive us? The death of a small child is virtually unthinkable to a parent. It almost defies logic. When it happens, you continue to exist, though walking the terrain of mere existence can be frightening. A dark abyss looms just ahead. You hesitate, wondering if the waters inside will swallow you up. And yet, again and again, you are drawn to the precipice. For you hear the whisper of some elusive promise of hope rising from the depths.

Questions haunted me day and night: *How had it happened? Why had it happened? Who was to blame? Why hadn't the hyena taken me instead? Did Garrit suffer? Where was he now? Was he all right? Would I ever see him again?* The answers lay in Africa, I thought, not at home in the States.

Staying on in Botswana for almost four months, I contacted hyena experts, police and wildlife officials investigating Garrit's death, the emergency-rescue crew, doctors who had examined the body, local safari operators and others who might be able to answer some of my questions. Though my search for answers was productive, I was vaguely aware that it was also a means to distract myself from looking the enormity of my loss in the eye. Still too raw to allow myself to feel the pain, I could only run from it.

I'd read enough to know that distraction and escape were not the typical prescriptions for healing one's grief. Nonetheless, I followed my impulses instead. In hindsight, I was still numb with shock. I'd drifted into the trauma survivor's eerie state of temporary detachment. My instinct for self-preservation impelled me to avoid the potentially overwhelming impact of grief for as long as I needed.

Though keeping busy usually kept the pain at bay, it sometimes seeped out with a life of its own. The sound of children's laughter and the sight of boys Garrit's age playing soccer was intolerable. Grocery shopping was an

ordeal: My eyes riveted upon the ice creams, puddings
and treats I used to buy for Garrit; every aisle contained
some food reminding me of his absence. It took stamina to
enter shopping malls: Halloween costumes on display,
books Garrit had loved and T-shirts just his size con-
fronted me like apparitions of ghosts.

I trained myself to ignore the giraffes, elephants and
warthogs drinking from the waterhole in front of the
wilderness chalet where I stayed. I hardly noticed the
long-legged ostriches chasing one another in circles, flapping their wings like cartoonish characters. The sight of
those creatures had delighted Garrit and me. Spellbound,
we'd watch them for hours. Now, I turned my back on
them.

If it weren't for the compassion and wisdom of others, I
might have ended up a brittle shell of a human being, my
sadness clamped tight inside, my capacity for joy a frail
memory.

A friend who invited me to spend a week with her in
the hinterlands was discerning enough simply to let me
be. Grateful, I breathed in the softness of the river and the
sound of fish eagles gliding like miniature planes on air,
then swooping through thickets of papyrus into the shallows after their prey.

A helicopter pilot accustomed to *National Geographic* pho-
tographers as passengers flew me for a small fee to the site
where Garrit was killed. Discreetly, he waited in the distance until I was ready to leave. During our flight back, he
told me that several years ago he'd witnessed his fiancée
die when her helicopter crashed. The subject of death did
not seem to embarrass him. Yet no more words were necessary. He understood that I needed to hold in my hands
the earth where my son had taken his final breath.

The young Indian woman who ran one of Botswana's
few Internet cafés and let me stay after-hours had lost her

eight-year-old son to an illness doctors had misdiagnosed. She told me that her life had never been the same. "Nine years have passed," she said, "but I still cry for him. The pain lessens, but you'll always live with the loss."

For the most part, people neither shied away from me, nor tried to console me with the empty platitudes considered appropriate expressions of sympathy in Western cultures: Your son is at peace; God is taking care of him; time heals; it's time to get on with your life.

Even the healers and Bushmen I contacted for answers to the more existential questions preoccupying me were fearlessly direct and humane. Why had such a terrible thing happened? I asked. It was his destiny, they said. When I probed further, their responses varied from the disconcerting to the wondrous. Bushmen elders felt that some antipathy had been unintentionally misdirected at Garrit, bewitching him. A reflexologist thought to be psychic believed that Garrit was one of the "indigo children" who would return to Earth during the next world cataclysm to ensure the survival of traditional cultures and peoples. Though I was skeptical of such concrete explanations, the possibility that Garrit had been destined to die for some purpose opened my mind to the prospect that there might be a meaning to what seemed a senseless death.

Healers invariably told me to face my pain. "Feel your heart break every day," one advised. "Only then will you begin to heal." A Bushman, placing his hands over my heart, told me that I hadn't finished crying. "You are in pain. Your son is worried about you. You must cry now, then stop. That way you can help your son." A white man who'd grown up in Botswana, who possessed a combination of bush wisdom and Western knowledge, took one look at me and said, "Your heart needs to cry more, to soften and feel the sorrow. Mourn for as long as you need to."

Intellectually, I understood the message that if I opened

my heart up and let myself feel the pain I'd been running from, a healing process would begin, which, in turn, might help Garrit. In retrospect, however, I wasn't ready to accept the wisdom behind the words. Only months after I'd returned home would I recognize that the seeds for healing lay within me. It would be up to me whether those seeds remained dormant or germinated.

I was ambivalent about returning home to Baltimore because I felt as if Garrit's spirit lived on in Botswana. Going home meant abandoning my child. It meant facing the myriad fragments of boyhood he'd left behind—his menagerie of cats, dogs, emus and cockatiels; the swings behind the house, soccer balls, basketballs, hockey sticks, old sneakers; Mother's Day letters he'd written over the years; books about Africa and wildlife we'd collected; the new bedroom I had built for him while we were away and that he'd never sleep in; the radio he hid under his pillow to listen to in secret after we'd said good night.

Despite my trepidation, I had to go home, if only temporarily. I could no longer pretend that the bank accounts I'd depleted during the months following Garrit's death would rejuvenate on their own. Moreover, recurring flashbacks haunting me day and night needed professional attention unavailable in Botswana.

Now, after having been in the States for fourteen months, I'd like to tell you that some cookie-cutter solution to grief worked like a magic balm. I'd like to say that the abyss of suffering looming before me was only a mirage.

I wish it were so simple. But grieving souls do not heal easily.

Going home turned out to be a rapid descent into hell. The familiarity of my surroundings only sharpened my awareness of Garrit's absence. Incomplete without him, I'd lost a vital part of my identity. Estranged from Garrit's father since our divorce years ago, and with little family to count upon for emotional support, I went into virtual isolation. There was only a handful of friends I'd see, and a psychiatrist who specialized in post-traumatic stress disorders. A stranger to myself, I felt as uncomfortable in most people's presence as I assumed they felt in mine.

I closed the curtains and stayed in bed for over a month, rousing myself twice a week for therapy. Days and nights merged into one another; time became irrelevant. I stopped answering the phone, stopped bathing, and began to swallow more pills and alcohol than food. Alternating between sleeping and crying, my eyes vanished into pockets of swollen flesh. My strength and inner resources shriveled. When I thought my body was shutting down, I no longer cared whether I lived or died.

I waited for destiny to step in and decide. It came in the form of two policemen with paperwork from the psychiatrist stating that I was no longer able to care for myself. Handcuffing me when I resisted, the police hauled me out of bed and drove me to the emergency room of a third-rate hospital. For twenty-four hours, wearing nothing but a scanty hospital gown, I lay motionless on a narrow bed in a windowless closet of a room. I felt like a spectator watching myself fade away, observing my spirit pass through my pores like air slipping quietly from a worn-out balloon.

Then, suddenly, I realized I wasn't meant to die this way. It wasn't my time to die. I'd been to hell and survived. I was alive for a reason, a purpose I sensed to be intertwined with Garrit's death.

When I stepped from the hospital into the world, I finally felt ready to find a way to live with the bundle of pain I carried inside. Shortly afterward, I left Baltimore and moved across the country to start life over in Santa Fe. There, I began to reconstruct the parts of my being most shattered by Garrit's death and to pare from my life all that seemed superfluous or false. As I came to feel more intact at some core level, a brittleness that had grown around my heart since Garrit's death seemed gradually to soften, as if preparing to fall away.

The process of reshaping my life will probably take years. At times, it feels like a painful rebirth, yet a rebirth that is necessary if I want to do more than exist. Although I've made a conscious decision to live, I have wondered what will prevent me from sinking again. I found that with the will to live came something that makes the unbearable more bearable. Difficult to name, I think of it as a whisper of promise coupled with grace. When the pain threatens to pull me under, that whisper keeps me afloat, lightening the weight of my sorrow, gracing me with a new sense of compassion for myself and others.

My life has irrevocably changed. I will never be the person I was. While I don't know who I will become or where my path will ultimately lead, the heartbreaking loss of my son will always remain a profound part of me. Yet, at the same time, the capacity to feel joy again is germinating inside; simple pleasures I used to take for granted have taken on new value. This paradoxical mixture of sorrow and promise seems to be the nature of the process of my grief and gradual rebirth.

Now, though winter reigns in Botswana, spring is here, greening the landscape. Children play outside, delighted with themselves. Crocuses and daffodils shout with color. With such abundance of rebirth in the air, it seems cruel that Garrit cannot return to life. There are moments when I want to stamp out the flowers, snap each bud in half and pretend that other people's children don't exist.

And yet, just today, I came upon a boy about Garrit's age and size humming quietly to himself as he drew lines into the soil with a stick. Though I felt the familiar clench of pain in my throat, instead of turning from the sight of that boy, for a second my heart softened. A fleeting smile passed between us, tracing a slender finger of hope across my flesh.

Molly Bruce Jacobs

Ashley's Garden

"Mommy, would you be sad if I died?" Disturbing words quickly tumbled from the mouth of four-year-old Ashley, taking her mother, Kathleen Treanor, by surprise.

"Of course, I would, Ashley. I'd miss you terribly."

"But don't be sad, Mommy. I'd be an angel watching over you."

With a wink and a promise to stay close by her side, childish giggles soon filled the air. Yes, everything was back on key, with no more talk of four-year-olds going to heaven before their time.

A few days later, Kathleen brought Ashley to Grandma LaRue's house. Grandma was a wonderful sitter, whose home overflowed with love, comfort and joy. Without a doubt, crafts and homemade cookies would soon be on their way.

After tenderly kissing Ashley good-bye, Kathleen jumped in her car and hurried off to work. She'd hardly arrived and settled comfortably in her chair, with a steaming cup of freshly brewed coffee, when she heard it. A huge blast rocked Oklahoma City, and just as quickly destroyed her world.

Confused and unsure of what happened, a coworker

flipped on the television. Everyone in the office stood in reverent shock as the news began to unfold. There'd been an enormous explosion at the Murrah Federal Building. Kathleen could hardly believe her eyes. *Not in my hometown,* she thought. *Not here!* Soon, young mothers were running back and forth in a frantic search for their children. Kathleen was horrified to discover there'd been a daycare in the building. *My God, the children,* she thought, as she began to pray for the desperate families.

Within moments, her sister called with unimaginable news, unraveling the last shred of Kathleen's protective shroud of peace. Luther and LaRue Treanor had taken Ashley to their social security appointment, which was inside the Murrah building. Suddenly, the room began to spin. Surreal humming filled Kathleen's ears. Ashley was in that devastated structure—the one she was watching on the news!

It took days to discover their complete loss. But slowly, the details came forth. Her mother-in-law and father-in-law, along with Ashley, were found among the dead. Kathleen immediately slipped into a deep, dark depression, not able to comprehend how evil minds could change the destiny of so many innocent souls.

But months later, Kathleen recalled a prayer she'd uttered just days before the bombing, pleading with God for a message of hope to share with a hurting world. Then her mind raced to Ashley's words just before the explosion, "Don't be sad if I die. I'll be an angel watching over you." Suddenly, Kathleen realized she was being prepared for a mission far beyond her understanding.

In gratitude for the peace only God offers, she planted a memorial for her daughter. Today, Ashley's Garden is adorned with a graceful weeping willow, a fountain and an abundance of lively, brilliant flowers. For all who see it, the message is clear. Life goes on. Joy follows sorrow. Light rises from darkness.

Through five years of journals and endless prayers, Kathleen's dream to see her daughter's legacy shared within the pages of the book *Ashley's Garden* have finally come to pass, and her prayer for a healing ministry has reached far beyond her dreams.

When Kathleen awoke on the morning of September 11, 2001, along with the rest of the world, she froze in disbelief. America had, once again, been struck by the evil of terrorism. In that moment, she knew, her words of hope and healing would reach far beyond the borders of Oklahoma. They would now take her to New York City.

So, along with survivors and victims' families, she boarded a plane and flew toward her destiny. It was there she saw the ultimate fulfillment of prayer as she escorted grieving individuals, one by one, to Ground Zero, beginning the long, but vital, process of healing. By meeting the Oklahomans, the people of New York were able to see firsthand that time and faith heal all wounds.

No one knows what the future holds, but for now, Kathleen's on a mission, reaching out to the hurting, the wounded and to all who grieve with an inspiring message of hope born of prayer.

And back in Oklahoma, Ashley's Garden still blooms.

Candy Chand

Two Answers to One Prayer

Steve Wilson is, like myself, a presenter of humor programs. When I interviewed him, Wilson told me about an incident that happened to him related to humor and grief.

"I had always gone out," he said, "to talk to community groups about standard psychological subjects—like marriage, divorce, raising kids, stress, depression and things like that. One day," Wilson continued, "I got a call from a woman at a cancer clinic who runs a group called Make Today Count. She heard that I give talks and asked that I come and address the group. I told her that I had a new talk on humor. She said, 'That would be wonderful. I think the group would really like that.'"

Wilson was excited to do it. His mother had died of ovarian cancer when he was twenty years old so he thought it would be great if he could be of some help to these people.

There were about thirty-five people seated in a circle that night. To get the meeting started each person told the group their name, the kind of cancer they had and the stage of treatment they were in.

The first person said, "My name is Susan. I have a brain tumor. They were able to do surgery, and now I'm getting radiation." Then Susan's parents introduced themselves. After that, a young man, who was also there with his parents, announced that he had lymphoma.

"I started to realize," Wilson admits, "the gravity of the situation these people were in—and there was a room full of them." As each person went around the room, Wilson started to feel inadequate and questioned whether it was right to discuss humor under such circumstances. "Here were people with really catastrophic illnesses in their lives. I worried that my program wasn't appropriate."

To ease his fears, Wilson said a prayer: "God, if this is where you want me to be and there is something in this message that you want these people to hear, then I hope this is the right thing and that you will help me in what I say."

The prayer was answered in two ways.

First, a man who was introducing himself to the group said, "My name is Lester, and I'm pissed off. I have cancer of the liver. My doctor told me I had six months to live. That was a year ago—and I gave away my winter coat."

When everyone in the group started to laugh, it was a validation for Wilson that the group wanted to laugh and that a person in a serious situation could indeed poke fun at himself.

With the knowledge that humor was indeed appropriate, Wilson started his talk. He told jokes, played with props and explained the value of humor. It was going well. The crowd was laughing loudly and really appreciating what Wilson was doing.

Then there was a knock on the door. A woman opened it and stuck her head in the room. She said, "Listen, I'm trying to run a support group in the room next door . . ." Wilson thought to himself, *Okay, now I'm in trouble.* But the woman continued, "and my group would like to come in and join your group."

It wasn't until after the program that Wilson found out that the second gathering was a support group for those who had recently lost a loved one.

This was the second answer to his prayer. "People who came together to support each other in their grief," says Wilson, "wanted to be where the laughter was."

Allen Klein, M.A., C.S.P.

Laugh and Let Go

Mirth is God's medicine.

Henry Ward Beecher

It's no secret that laughter can be a healer. In *Anatomy of an Illness as Perceived by the Patient,* Norman Cousins describes how laughter healed his cancer—and it can heal grief.

Aunt Lucy had an iron will, a sharp tongue and a reputation as a penny-pincher. Nothing was ever wasted. Wrapping paper was smoothed out and neatly refolded. String was wound onto an ever-enlarging ball. Aluminum foil had an afterlife that would turn Shirley MacLaine green with envy.

Lucy's niece, Barbara, lived with and cared for Aunt Lucy after her own mother's death. While there was a loving bond between them, it was often expressed sharply, through biting humor. Each had a long list of things they found intolerable about the other.

"You're cheap!" accused Barbara.

"You're a spendthrift!" snapped Aunt Lucy.

Their good-natured bickering went on and on, adding spice to their afternoon tea.

In her declining years, Aunt Lucy began to plan for that great day when she would (as she put it) "meet her maker." Most of the planning concerned what she would wear to her funeral. As time passed, she became almost fixated on her choice of lingerie. She had always been a staunch and vocal advocate of clean undergarments. All the usual reasons were given, including windy streets and, most popular, being struck down by a bus and rushed to the hospital where—heaven forbid!—doctors and nurses would be forced to stop all lifesaving measures in the presence of less-than-perfect panties.

Week after week Aunt Lucy traveled to the shopping mall where she purchased lacy unmentionables in which to meet her maker. At first this seemed harmless enough, but it wasn't long before this diversion took the proportions of an outright obsession.

Underwear fueled the fire between Barbara and Aunt Lucy. They argued about it night and day. Aunt Lucy was fiercely determined to meet God Almighty in the best undies money could buy; Barbara, nerves frayed and patience dwindling, was just as determined to have Aunt Lucy carted away to the loony bin.

I had tea with them one afternoon and tried to smooth the waters. Barbara was close to her breaking point as we walked together in the garden.

"Barbara," I said gently, "Lucy's a wonderful old lady who's scared of dying. All she dares to focus on is how she will look when she has to stand before the Pearly Gates and explain why all her life she pinched pennies until they howled. Give her a break and try to smile about it. You don't really care about the money she's spending, do you?"

"Of course I don't," said Barbara, smiling. "It's just so

silly, and she won't see it. For years she's played eccentric, but she knew it and had a twinkle in her eye about it. But this—this is too serious."

"Death is serious, especially if you're terrified of it. And I think Aunt Lucy is terrified, despite the bluff."

"What can I do?" sighed Barbara.

"Join the fun." I put my arm around her shoulder, and she leaned her head against it.

"I'll try," she promised.

During the next few weeks Barbara helped Aunt Lucy with her shopping. They laughed together as the dresser drawers filled to bursting with lingerie. Finally, they narrowed the selection to seven pairs to eventually choose from. They put them in a beautiful, scented box to await that special day. It came sooner than either of them expected. Perhaps, having made her selection, Aunt Lucy felt comfortable about going to meet her maker.

I attended the wake. Aunt Lucy looked beautiful in her gray wool Chanel suit and her mother's pearls. Her white-gloved hands held her worn Bible.

"You don't think she looks . . . er . . . stout?" asked Barbara.

"Stout? No, why?" I wondered what she was getting at.

"Good. I was afraid she might. She hadn't made her final lingerie selection before she died. We'd narrowed it down to seven ensembles but . . ." she lowered her voice, "you know how fussy she was. I decided to let her make the final choice."

"Are you saying what I think you're saying?" my mind reeled.

"I had her dressed in all seven of them," Barbara winked. "She can choose when she gets there."

Ted Menten

My Grief Is Like a River

My grief is like a river—
I have to let it flow,
But I myself determine
Just where the banks will go.

Some days the current takes me
In waves of guilt and pain,
But there are always quiet pools
Where I can rest again.

I crash on rocks of anger—
My faith seems faith indeed,
But there are other swimmers
Who know that what I need

Are loving hands to hold me
When the waters are too swift,
And someone kind to listen
When I just seem to drift.

Grief's river is a process
Of relinquishing the past.
By swimming in hope's channels
I'll reach the shore at last.

Cynthia G. Kelley
Reprinted from the January 1988 issue of Bereavement *magazine*

Legacy of Love

On November 29, 1999, our son Jarod ended his life. With his death our world changed forever. What followed this tragic loss was an incredibly difficult journey, as our family was plunged into an abyss of grief.

We had no concept, until then, what grief really was and how difficult a journey it could be. In the beginning, it was hard just to get through a day; the four of us were all grieving at different points. Our home was in total chaos. We didn't know how to help each other, because we were so wrapped up in our own grief, not realizing that, as a family, this process would be ongoing for the rest of our lives!

In the beginning, it was as if we were suspended in time. The situation was unbelievably devastating. It was extremely difficult to focus on the simplest of details, as our thoughts were constantly of our loss.

As time goes on, we have found that the bouts of immense sadness have come further apart and for shorter periods of time. We are learning to deal with the void that Jarod's death has left in our lives.

Often, the stigma of suicide rests heavily on those left behind. Who are we to judge? We feel our reaction as a society should be one of love, not judgment. Is it fair that all the kind acts and good impressions of our son be forgotten and blotted out by his final, tragic act? This is terribly sad. Jarod was a very kindhearted and caring young man. There were no warnings of any kind, resulting in total devastation for his family and the community. Jarod was a freshman in college who worked part-time, and was active in the community coaching his brother's baseball and soccer teams. He was respected and loved by many, both young and old. So we ask, "What happened?" Were we too busy loving him (and he loving us) not to see any warning signs? There were no outward signs at all. He tried to protect us even to the very end and beyond.

We are eternally thankful to have had the opportunity to have been his parents. We bear no shame in that Jarod ended his own life. We are extremely proud of the person he was while here on Earth with us.

We now know that a time will come when the days of joy from having time to spend with Jarod will overshadow the sorrow of the brief time and apparent unfairness of his death. We feel that life is a gift, and whatever time we have, however brief that may be, should be utilized to enrich the lives of others. Events occur throughout our lives for no apparent reasons—destiny, as some will say. We simply need to have faith, and we don't need to know why in order to have acceptance. We believe that there are forces that bring us into being for a particular purpose. However, we do sometimes choose a different path, as is evidenced by our son's tragic decision.

Jarod's time with us was brief, yet very meaningful, as he made many positive and lasting impressions on all those he came in contact with. He glowed brightly and intensely, and therefore used up his light more quickly than others. He felt certain that we would understand, and on many levels we do. We have focused not on his choice to remove himself from life, but rather on the incredibly positive influence he was on all those lives that he touched. It is also important for us to remain focused on the fact that Jarod will live on in our hearts forever. We feel that Adam and Lori will have a great deal of difficulty with the loss of their brother. For them, it feels as though he chose to leave them behind, and that is very difficult to understand. A parent has gained a very different perspective on life in the first place, having been an instrument in creating it and having had to learn to accept its mortal quality right from the beginning. For us, there was a time without Jarod before his birth. For Adam and Lori, there was never a time without him, until now. So older siblings and parents seem so permanent. It's a rude awakening to discover that they are not!

Our friend, Holly, who also lost her son to suicide, had told us of her desire to craft a patchwork quilt made with her son's clothing. Inspired by these thoughts, we also felt moved to assemble a quilt after sorting through Jarod's clothes. It was extremely difficult to bring his clothes back into our home. As we touched and smelled his earthly garments, we shed tears of sadness and joy, recalling memories of Jarod attached to each piece.

Assembling the quilt became the first step toward passing through our grieving process, as we knew it would be very easy to stay stuck in the grief. Instead we put that grief to work in a positive way that we hope can inspire others who have suffered a horrific loss. Stitched together, grief, healing and remembrance became the quilt that we refer to as our "Legacy of Love."

Over a period of about five months, we stitched the pieces of Jarod's life together in a magnificent work of art—a quilt in his memory. The project became a balm that has helped to ease our bereavement. With every stitch, the horrible rift has gradually mended, easing shock, disbelief and pain. Our quilt is distinctly different from traditional handcrafted pieces. Each block is a unique representation of a different facet of Jarod's life. Every stitch stands as a tribute to an outstanding young man with a ready smile and a passion for any activity he embraced.

For months, I sat at my machine cutting, piecing and sewing. As the family watched the process, they decided to design their own personal squares. Jarod's dad, Ed, assembled a square that features suspenders, matching tie and a white shirt inclusive of the buttons and pocket, a valued gift from him to Jarod. Lori, who is Jarod's younger sister, chose one of Jarod's shirts. She used it as a backdrop for photographs of the two of them together throughout their lives. Adam, Jarod's younger brother, added a letter he wrote to his brother the summer before, thanking him for being the best big brother a boy could ever have in life, and the cover from a baseball they used to throw around together. To this legacy of love, we added car keys, attire Jarod wore, pictures of family members, his favorite baseball cap and much more.

Crafting the quilt caused many raw emotions to surface. But doing so helped our family to cope with our grief in the best possible way—as a family. We know this quilt has really helped us a great deal with the healing. We tried to put his whole life into the quilt. Finally, at the end of June 2000, the quilt was finished just in time for what would have been Jarod's nineteenth birthday. Friends and family were invited to our home for a special quilt signing. They added memories and messages to the back of the quilt. Our home was full all day long. When people came into our home, we could see the "Oh, I remember when he wore this" expressions. The memories aren't just for us; they are also for others who knew and loved him.

We feel some sense of relief from the grief since the completion of our quilt, and now we want to share it in hopes that our story will help to inspire other families who are in the process of grieving. This "Legacy of Love" we created and our memories of Jarod are all that we have left as evidence of his brief life. We keep our memory-laden quilt on the back of our couch, so that when we feel the need for a hug, we can wrap ourselves in the quilt and feel him with us once again.

Ed and Sandra Kervin

Chris's Funeral

After Chris's funeral our friends gathered at the house where Chris had been living to share some stories, drink some beers and celebrate the life of my brother. There were many tender moments that night as we traded our favorite of Chris's sayings or the funniest things that he did, but nothing touched me more than a tribute that was made without words.

John lived in our neighborhood growing up, and he and Chris were best friends, lifelong friends. They both loved to play their guitars and listen to the Rolling Stones. John was talented and dedicated to playing the guitar. Chris was less talented, but he was determined to learn to play well. Their paths split after high school while John was putting in endless hours of practice and Chris was out pursuing dreams that held more promise for him than music. He knew that he did not have the natural ability that John did, but he always loved the idea of being a guitar player. He loved the fact that John was making a living playing his guitar.

When Chris was twenty-seven, he moved to Atlanta and began a new job. He bought a new electric guitar with his signing bonus, one with a maple neck, one he had wanted for years. He called John to tell him about it.

After Chris died, I thought about his things and what we should do with them. When I thought about his new guitar and his amplifier, I thought of John. I knew that Chris would want John to have his guitar, because no one would appreciate it and use it as much as John would. No one would know what it meant to Chris as much as John would. I called John and told him that we wanted him to have the guitar, and he was touched. I told him to get it after the funeral.

John, his wife Audrey, and their new baby daughter, Ellie, were at our gathering after Chris's funeral. After an hour or two had passed, I wondered if they were still at the house. I hadn't seen them in a while. I walked upstairs to the room Chris had been staying in to see if John remembered to take the guitar with him when he left. As I got to the top of the stairs, I heard the sound of music coming from Chris's room. I tapped gently on the door and stepped into the room.

Audrey and Ellie were silently lying next to each other on the bed. As I walked in, Audrey sat up on one elbow and smiled sympathetically at me. John was sunken into Chris's chair next to the bed. His eyes were closed. He held Chris's maple-necked guitar in his lap, and he was quietly playing the blues. His head was tilted back, and tears were squeezing out of the corners of his eyes and sliding heavily down the contours of his face. John worked his fingers along the neck of the guitar, and he made it sing about how he was feeling. The chords ran deeply through me.

He wasn't doing it for me; he was doing it because there was no better way to show and share his emotion with his family and with Chris. He was in Chris's room on Chris's guitar; he was playing with him one last time, and he was expressing his pain.

In simple words, it was a grand tribute. It was one of the most touching moments of my life, and I will never forget the feeling that I got from John making that guitar wail so quietly and sweetly. My presence in the room only lasted a few minutes, but the meaningful expression from those few minutes will stay with me for the rest of my life.

Scott Michael Mastley

Grieving Time, a Time for Love

If a loved one has departed,
And left an empty space,
Seek the inner stillness,
Set a slower pace.
Take time to remember,
Allow yourself to cry,
Acknowledge your emotions,
Let sadness pass on by.
Then center in the oneness,
Remember . . . God is here,
Death is but a change in form,
Your loved one is still near.
Treat yourself with kindness,
Allow yourself to feel,
God will do the mending,
And time will help you heal.

Barbara Bergen

The Letter

My fingers went numb when I received the call that my brother Bob had died. How could this happen to a forty-eight-year-old who never drank or smoked and went to church every Sunday? I spent that entire evening sitting in solitude and reflecting on all the things we did together growing up. The tears that soaked my pillow that night made me question my own mortality. The nervousness that greeted me in the morning left me with the unanswered question, "Why Bob?" The only thought that made sense was that everything happens for a reason, and God must have needed him badly. A fatal heart attack while vacationing with his wife in Hawaii? The entire day I wallowed in self-pity and disbelief. I went to work and shared the horrendous news. I wondered whether I was ever going to shake the fear that life isn't fair and how I could get through this. I went with my brother Mark after work to Bob's house to see what we could do. Bob's three surviving children, Tammy (twenty-five), Jenny (twenty-four) and Andy (nineteen), were home alone wondering what happened to their dad and why. Besides, I needed something to do to keep busy.

When we arrived, we found Tammy shaking and

trembling in the passenger seat of her friend's car. Jenny was crying uncontrollably as she approached us with a big hug. We found Andy sitting in the backyard gazebo after we were warned he hadn't spoken a word since getting the news. It was at that moment that I realized I didn't just lose my brother, but my sweet nieces and nephew had just lost their dad.

Somehow I started to relax. This was no longer about me and my sorrow. This was about trying to make a difference and helping them. Clearly, I didn't have a clue about what to say, but if I just kept talking, something might make them feel better. I began sharing my memories of how I felt when my dad died. I tried to be positive and reflect how lucky I was that he was supportive and just the kind of dad I always wanted. How after sharing these thoughts with my friends, they began expressing how lucky I was that I had such a wonderful childhood and that their experience was not as fortunate.

At the funeral I overheard a conversation my mom was having with Tammy. I turned around just in time to hear Tammy ask, "Nana, when I feel up to it, can I come over to your house sometime and maybe you can tell me about my dad growing up and what he was like?"

"Absolutely!" Mom warmly replied.

It was at that moment when I realized how I could help. A part of me felt like I was interrupting a private conversation, but I turned to Tammy and asked, "Can I write you a letter and tell you about your dad?"

"Uncle Jim, would you do that? That would be great." Somehow I felt like I was contributing to filling in the pieces they figured they'd always have time to assemble. Word spread quickly to Jenny and Andy of my offer to all three of them. For the next three weeks during lunch, I found a quiet spot and began to write. I didn't really intend on saying too much, but after the first day my memories of growing up with Bob seemed special. I spoke of the times we were kids, and he always wanted to walk to the store singing all the way there and back. He always loved to sing the harmony parts. And you know what? By the time we got home the song sounded pretty good. I had no idea my mental stroll would ignite such profound memories.

For some reason, my wanting to help my nieces and nephew became a warm recollection for myself. I began outlining the major events of our childhood—things I remembered him doing—the trouble he used to get into—the silly things he did to embarrass himself. I didn't need the kids to think of their dad as perfect. I wanted them to know that we were kids one time, making mistakes, learning from them and then moving on. By the time I was done writing, there were eleven pages. I couldn't believe all the things I had to say. I put each letter along with a childhood photo of their dad and me in a manila envelope and printed their name on the front. I was proud of the effort I hoped somehow could help. What I didn't count on was what a difference it made for me. A simple gesture of sharing information to heal their hearts actually helped me to heal mine.

I drove to their house one Saturday afternoon, and unfortunately, they weren't there. I dropped three envelopes inside the door and left. Weeks went by, and I never heard a word. It didn't matter. At the end of the letter I actually thanked them for letting me share my memories of their dad growing up and how much this meant to me. How my heart was filled with smiling thoughts of a brother who died much too soon. I was proud I had developed my writing skills to accurately describe my thoughts to them. I was ready to move on and in some way to help them do the same. I reassured all three how I would always be there and that I was always only a phone call away.

A few months later I got a letter from Jenny, who had returned to college. She wrote that she had been too hurt to read my letter and was waiting for the right time when she felt stronger. One day she was missing her dad and family and began to read. She wrote how it was just what she needed at the perfect time. What meant the most to me was that she was planning on thanking me with an e-mail but she said nothing short of a personal letter back to me was acceptable—that if the day ever came when I wanted to remember my importance to her I could pull out the letter and read it.

I wiped a proud tear away and quietly put the letter in my scrapbook of souvenirs. For it's in these moments that I realize what life is all about.

And death.

Jim Schneegold

A Firehouse Christmas

We must not, in trying to think about how we can make a big difference, ignore the small daily differences we can make which, over time, add up to big differences that we often cannot foresee.

Marion Wright Edelman

*... she stood
in the station doorway
framed by snowflakes
the size of a toddler's hand.
Heavy, white ones,
falling like tiny angels
who couldn't resist a short dance in her hair.
Like Santa she brought joy,
Her bulging bundle of teddy bears
and woolly mammoths,
their faces pressed
against the opaque bag,
hoping for escape,
a chance to be squeezed again*

by little hands, and
held close to tiny faces ...

Seattle Decembers are misty and steel gray, like the navy ships and aircraft carriers that silently ply our waterways. Three or four times each winter a heavy, wet Puget Sound snow bends the cedar boughs and hemlock branches and the carpet of ferns on the forest floor with white wonder. It blankets and crusts our curving, winding roadways, turning every hill into a toboggan course for kids and the adults who wish they still were.

For a fire-station lieutenant, it also fills the nights with fender benders, abandoned vehicles and power outages. I get precious little sleep on snowy shifts, but the joy our icy visitor brings to children is worth the commotion and confusion.

The pre-Christmas snow assault had been underway for two hours, and my station had already responded to three rush-hour accidents. Fresh coffee was brewing. All indicators pointed to a sleepless, hectic night. I was sure the knock on the firehouse door was a stranded motorist or a passerby reporting yet another accident on the busy four lane just beyond our station ramp. I was wrong.

I guessed her to be about thirty-five. She was a slightly built, auburn-haired woman who stood outside the doorway, smiling through the silver-dollar-sized flakes of snow. I invited her in and offered her the first sampling of our firehouse brew, making her laugh out loud with my comment about not having a sharp knife handy to cut it. She accepted my offer, kicking the crusted snow off her boots as she entered. She lugged a bulging, kitchen-size garbage bag in her left hand, leaning slightly out of balance to compensate for its weight.

She shook the snow out of her hair and blew on her hands while I poured a cup of the pungent firehouse java.

"What do you take in it?" I said over my shoulder.

"Just black, thanks," she replied.

I carried the two steaming cups across the kitchen and handed one to her. She wrapped both hands around the warm mug, smiled and thanked me. Between sips we speculated as to whether or not the early snow meant a brutal winter bearing down on us. She laughed again when I told her I was going to make a ton of extra money by setting up a chain- and stud-installation service outside our bay doors.

I looked down at her white plastic bag. She must have seen the question flicker across my face because she smiled and answered before I could ask. "I couldn't bring myself to come here for the first three years," she began. Her voice trembled a little as she spoke. "I'm sorry it's taken me so long to say 'thank you' but, well, here I am."

The picture was clearer now, yet I still didn't have all the puzzle pieces. "Ma'am?"

She tilted her head and motioned, gesturing toward the bag she'd placed gently on the entryway tile. "These were my son's." Protruding from the top of the bag was a buck-toothed, charcoal-brown beaver. Below the beaver I could see an assortment of two dozen stuffed animal toys. They looked like a band of mutinous zoo critters preparing for a breakout.

When she told me her son's name, the last puzzle piece fit. He had been another victim on our highway several years ago—another heartbreaking loss, a child we couldn't save. He had died just prior to the holidays. I can't imagine there ever being a good time for your child to die, but it seems having to endure such a devastating loss as holidays approach would add a final twist of cruelty.

For a moment, words failed me. I could think of nothing to say, so I said nothing. I stared at the droplets of moisture in her hair. She took a deep breath, smiled and said, "I can't find a use for these now, so I was wondering if you could give them away." She paused. "I mean, to kids who need them."

Like many other fire departments, our medic units carry a supply of stuffed animals. When a child is hurt or sick, a teddy bear may not ease the pain, but it brings comfort. It's a buddy who understands and who doesn't complain if he's squeezed too tight. This woman knew about our teddy bear giveaway program, and she was offering a very special collection.

I thought about asking "Are you sure?" but didn't. The look in her eyes told me she hadn't arrived at her decision lightly. "Thank you," I said. I thought carefully, then added, "I don't think you'll ever know how many little folks you'll touch by doing this."

"I hope you're right," she said. "I'm sure he'll be happy to know he's sharing with someone who needs help."

"Not gonna finish that coffee?" I asked. She was already heading for our front door, leaving the still steaming, half-full cup next to mine on the table. "Nope. I need to get home before it really gets bad."

I held the door open for her and told her to drive safely. She laughed again and said, "I'd better. I don't wanna be your next patient!" She paused for a second, turned and said, "Thank you."

I waved and responded, "Thank YOU! And Merry Christmas!"

The station tones went off again, this time dispatching my rescue crew to a woman in labor. Forty seconds later the white and blue medic unit rocketed out of the station and onto the highway, its blazing twin sonic beacons reflecting off the swirling snow. Alone, I returned to my coffee and the bag of stuffed animals.

I knelt beside it, pulling the furry little creatures out one by one. A stuffed hippo, a green and purple teddy bear, and a bald eagle with an extraordinarily large beak and limp wings that wrapped around his torso.

I wondered how many memories the bag contained. How many times a little boy had drifted off to sleep, cradling one. How many had heard a childhood secret whispered, how many a bedtime prayer? I thought of my son, A. J., and his collection of stuffed dinosaurs. In this mother's situation, could I, would I ever have the courage to give such precious mementos away? I gathered the stuffed animals and put them back into the bag, then placed it carefully in our supply room. The next morning I told the oncoming crew about our new supply of cuddlies.

The days are getting shorter again, the nights colder, and the holidays are approaching. It's been almost a year since that mom gave us her unique gift. I haven't spoken to her since. She hasn't stopped by or called. But if she does, I know exactly what I'm going to tell her.

I'll tell her about the nine-year-old little girl whose house burned. She never let go of that gray hippopotamus. Or the ten-year-old whose leg was shattered in three places after being thrown from a horse. At first he didn't want the brown and white beagle, but five minutes later was clutching it tightly against his chest. And the snow-white teddy bear we gave the five-year-old with a 104-degree fever. We named it Fritz, and it made a sick little boy smile.

Those are only the stories I know. There are many I haven't heard and probably never will. I know this: With each stuffed animal there is a special story made possible by a mother's gift of love. A tale of adversity, of pain and fear, interwoven with a strand of comfort only a stuffed animal could bring. For each toy a woman's son once cradled, there is now a rainbow in another family's storm. Could there be a more perfect way to chisel your child's legacy on the walls of history?

Aaron Espy

Grief Helps Others

Grief knits two hearts in closer bonds than happiness ever can; and common sufferings are far stronger links than common joys.

Alphonse de Lamartine

Linda Maurer studies a framed portrait of a beautiful young woman with long blonde hair and striking hazel eyes—her only child, Molly, who died in a railroad accident in the spring of 1991 when she was only nineteen.

She rereads the article she clipped from the newspaper about another mother's child who died tragically. Her eyes fill with tears as she puts pen to paper.

"I understand your grief because it happened to me," she writes to these suffering parents whom she has never met. "Let others help you through your terrible nightmare," she advises them. "You'll get stronger with each passing year, but you'll never, ever stop loving your child with all your heart."

Linda's love for her daughter was boundless. But she and Molly were also best friends. They went clothes shopping together and baked poppy-seed cakes and regularly waged battle on one of the local tennis courts. "You two are inseparable," friends often commented, and Linda always smiled and thanked God for blessing her with such a lively and loving child.

"I'm the only one in the dorm who can't wait for parents' weekend," Molly once told Linda on the phone from Arizona State University, where she was a freshman.

It was a few months later when Molly went on a spring-break train trip through Mexico with friends. There was a terrible accident. That Sunday afternoon Linda and Larry received the fateful phone call.

"Is it Molly?" Linda gasped when Larry's face turned white as a sheet, and she nearly passed out when he nodded yes. "Is she dead?" she asked, but deep in her heart Linda could already sense the answer. In the blink of an eye her precious Molly was gone.

"I simply can't bear this pain," Linda sobbed as mourners gathered at the family's Boulder, Colorado, home to offer their condolences and love. Dozens arrived from Molly's college. Others traveled from as far away as Australia to express their grief and to attend the funeral that filled a twelve-hundred-seat church to overflowing.

Neighbors brought food to feed the scores of mourners who gathered each day to pay their respects. Others cleaned and shopped and chauffeured Linda and Larry wherever they needed to go. Neither was in any shape to drive.

Linda cried herself to sleep. "I'll never see Molly graduate from college and begin a career," she grieved. "I'll never see her fall in love or start a family of her own."

The pain was so unbearable that Linda became briefly suicidal. But her friend Kay took Linda in hand. "See those kids?" she said, pointing to Molly's many friends who had gathered to share their tears and their memories. "If you take your own life, how many of them do you suppose might follow you? And what about Larry? He needs you just as much as you need him. The two of you must face this tragedy together."

Linda tried, but for months she was unable to bear the sight of any of Molly's favorite places: the local mall, the lake where the family used to go fishing, the tennis courts where Linda first taught her little girl how to swing a racket.

Once, when she felt strong enough to venture out to buy a friend a birthday card, Linda bolted from the shop in tears. "The racks were filled with Mother's Day cards," she wept that night in Larry's arms.

The holidays were hardest of all. Molly's birthday. Thanksgiving. Christmas.

It was the day after Christmas when Linda spotted a newspaper account of a young boy who had perished in a holiday skiing accident. Her heart went out to the child's mom and dad, and soon Linda was pouring out her feelings in a letter. "If there's anything we can do, please call," she urged, and a few weeks later the boy's parents came for a visit.

"How do you go on?" the newly bereaved mom asked Linda in a tear-choked voice.

Linda clasped Larry's hand. "We help each other," she explained. "It's the only way."

Linda's words seemed to comfort the couple, and from that day forward whenever Molly's mom heard of a child who had died she always took time to send the parents a heartfelt letter. The writing brought Linda solace, and many of those who received her notes called or wrote back to say how much her gentle words had helped them through their darkest hours.

One morning Linda awoke from hugging Molly in a dream with a single thought resounding in her head. "I'm going to write a book," she decided. She borrowed a typewriter and began that very afternoon. She described the sudden triggers of grief and loss, and how she and Larry finally found the strength to start living again. "Helping others is what God means for me to do with my life," Linda realized with sudden clarity.

Linda wrote not one book but two: *I Don't Know How to Help Them*, for friends and family of bereaved parents, and *Standing Beside You*, which she wrote for grieving moms and dads. She self-published both books and included her home address so anyone who wanted could contact her.

Soon the letters began pouring in, and they haven't stopped to this day. Linda answers each and every correspondence personally. She also attends book signings and organizes discussion groups afterward.

"When Molly died, I used to think that if she'd never lived, I wouldn't have to go through all of this pain," Linda shares with these groups. "But now I understand that I also would have missed out on the happiest, most fulfilling nineteen years of my life being Molly's mom."

These meetings always take their toll on Linda. Afterward, she lies awake for several nights, haunted by all the sad stories she's heard, and because she knows that for many of the parents she met, the real pain is only beginning.

Linda spends several hours every day at her desk answering the dozens of letters she receives each week from bereaved parents, their friends and their families. "If I can help one person get through another twenty-four hours, I know that my Molly is proud of me," she says. "She's with me always. She's standing right here beside me, and the memories don't hurt anymore."

Heather Black

Let the Body Grieve Itself

You don't think you'll live past it and you don't really. The person you were is gone. But the half of you that's still alive wakes up one day and takes over again.

Barbara Kingsolver

I woke up early on January 1, the first day of the new century, and crawled out of my cave (the name I have given to my bed). It had been an uneventful New Year's Eve, in bed by 10 P.M., pillow over my ears to block out the sounds of centennial celebrations in my neighborhood.

I had spent the past several years at the bottom of pain after my twenty-one-year-old daughter, Jenna, was killed in a bus accident while studying abroad. Her death and that of three other students on the bus in India had made news all around the world. I was a heartsick father, convinced there was nothing further to celebrate, ever. I went through the motions of trying to put my world back together. I acted as if my life would one day have purpose and meaning again, but I lived in utter despair. My life, as I had known it, was over. There would be no "good times," no celebrations, not without my daughter.

As I stepped over Rascal, the family dog, nestled in her spot bedside the bed, the phone rang. It was my friend Anne, in a panic and asking for my help. "Ken, I'm worried about Howard. He's been depressed all week. Would you please call him, Ken? Today?"

And so it was that I called my buddy Howard, whose third-generation family business was losing millions of dollars and facing a hostile takeover. Howard was glad to hear from me. In response to my invitation to go to lunch, he said, "I am on my way to yoga. Why don't you join me and then we can go for lunch?" Realizing I could help a friend in trouble and escape my own misery for a few hours, I agreed.

An hour later I was sitting lotus style next to Howard in a room full of bright-eyed yoga students. A surprising number of them were men my age who appeared to be in very good shape, and I began to wonder what I had gotten myself into. I could not remember the last time I had stretched; I had been filling my emptiness with food since Jenna's death and had gained twenty-five pounds. I also felt a little awkward sitting among a group of straight-backed, New Age types who obviously knew what they were doing. Then I gazed over at my friend, his face full of anguish, and he looked back at me, trying to smile. I was quickly reminded why I was there. I felt somehow closer to him than ever before, like he was beginning to understand what it was like to have your heart ripped out. I felt somehow less alone.

As the class settled in, a beautiful, young, soft-spoken yoga teacher named Diane invited us to turn our attention inward. She asked us to "find a comfortable position, close your eyes. Take a deep breath in, and on the out breath, release any tension you might be holding." Weaving a barefoot path through the mire of students, Diane then spoke the first of what would be many words I would never forget. "Let go! Trust. Let the body breathe itself."

What? I thought.

My breathing had become shallow and controlled. My pain was often so big, I did not know whether I could make it to the next moment. I had been fighting just to survive. And yet, listening to Diane's soft, reassuring voice, I was able to surrender a little bit at a time. *Let the body breathe itself,* I repeated over and over until I could feel myself soften and then let go. My body had been frozen by the trauma of my daughter's death. Each cell had been turned inside out. In a way, I too had died, had ceased to breathe. But here I was sitting on a yoga mat, discovering new breath, new movement and new life.

Diane then led us into a yoga posture she called "the heart opener."

Before I was able to fully grasp what my body was doing, I had let out a soft, harrowing sigh. Then I felt tears running down my cheek. In its wisdom, my body was allowing a small release. I had discovered a new cave, a safe, five-thousand-year-old refuge for my grief called "yoga." In the next hour, Diane's soothing voice led me on a gentle journey back into my body, my heart and my soul. The more she guided us, saying things like, "Let yourself in, gently, compassionately, without straining," the more I realized how I had locked myself out. I had shut down my body and emotions. Without really being aware of it, I was dying. Perhaps like many parents who experience the unspeakable, unthinkable nightmare of losing a child, I had shut down as a means of coping with the seemingly unending pain. And I had given up.

Guided and encouraged by a wise and caring teacher, I took my first baby steps. I began to learn the practice of self-compassion. And I had discovered a path to begin healing my life. Yoga taught me to reopen my heart and still my mind. Diane's invitations to "notice how your body is different each day" and "differentiate between tension and strength" taught me more about grief, healing and the rebirth of hope than any book I had read. I began to find nourishment in silence and felt somehow more connected with my daughter in those moments. At the end of that first class, as we sat silently, I spoke to Jenna, telling her that I loved her, that I was going to try to fight my way back into life and make her proud of me for not giving up. In the weeks and months to follow, I learned to calm the obsessive thinking that so often accompanies traumatic loss and to reactivate the "fight back" and "feel good" systems in my body. With coaching, I slowly learned that it was okay to allow grief to move through me. *Let the body grieve itself,* I began to tell myself.

It became a ritual for me to gently place my hand over my heart and cry softly for several moments during each class and to talk to Jenna during the closing meditations. I was clearing the way for a new life, one in which I could live with and through my loss. I would always grieve the death of my daughter. Now I could experience the joy and privilege of having had her in my life for twenty-one precious years. She would be in my heart forever. Since that day, I have attended yoga classes two or three times a week. I am gradually learning to live within my own skin again. I now accept that my grief is as choiceless as breathing. It cannot be forced or resisted, but it can be allowed. And I teach this to other parents each day through The Jenna Druck Foundation's Families Helping Families Program. I keep myself in top shape through yoga, physically, mentally and spiritually, and honor my daughter by walking with bereaved parents, brothers, sisters, relatives and friends as they find their way through the darkness that is grief.

I thought I was saving a friend's life by going to a New Year's Day yoga class. It turns out, it's my own life I saved.

Ken Druck

4

THOSE WE WILL MISS

What we have once enjoyed, we can never lose. All that we love deeply becomes a part of us.

Helen Keller

Father's Day

Good morning! Good morning! The song from a Beatles album issued a wake-up call to the morning radio-show listeners. As the raucous noise of horns, crowing roosters, yowling cats and barking dogs slowly died away, John Hancock, the host of the talk show, announced with his usual up-tempo enthusiasm, "It is a good morning! It's a Wednesday, and I don't feel like talking about the news. Most of my regular listeners out there know there are other things on my mind these days besides health-care reform in Charlotte, crime legislation in Raleigh and serial killers all grouped in the same sentence. So today is Father's Day—even though it's only March. I'll be back to explain." The music of melodious guitars changed the mood as Dan Fogelberg's song, "The Leader of the Band," filled the airwaves. And listeners heard the emotional words of a mournful son who not only denied his love for his father, but made a poor attempt to imitate the man he admired most.

The music faded and Hancock came back saying, "Yeah, I know. It can't be Father's Day. But you know—it's my show. Today, I want to pull your minds away from world dilemmas. Let's talk about something we all have in

common: fathers. Today, I promise I won't be rude. I won't
be arrogant. That's a switch, huh? I want you to call in and
introduce us to your dad. Living, dead, good and bad. Tell
us about that day with him at Shea Stadium, or remember
back to the best conversation you ever had with him. I
want to know what he taught you and why he's special.
Tell me about the dad who didn't leave when things got
tough. I don't know how energetic you're gonna get on
this subject but I hope it works. I'd hate to have to play
Montovani all day long. We'll take a break—the lines are
open. Back to you in two."

In seconds, all lines were jammed. He was a morning
talk-show host on the three-call-letter radio station in
North Carolina. The association with his audience could
best be described as a love/hate relationship. Most loved
him for his persuasive personality and gregarious sense of
humor and were tolerant of his attitude. But even those
who adamantly disagreed with him on many subjects and
disliked his arrogance couldn't resist listening to him. This
show would not be about complaints, whining or petti-
ness. The fifty thousand watts of air would be filled with
real stories from the hearts of his audience as they called
in testaments to their fathers.

The first caller said, "John, my father couldn't read or
write. He taught us ways to live that had nothing to do
with the three Rs. Honesty, respect and character are his
values. The whole family taught him to read when he was
sixty. He's a proud, yet humble guy who listens to you
every day. He's seriously ill now so before I miss the
chance—I'd like to say on the air, 'Dad, I love you,'" the
voice cracked in emotion.

A fragile female voice said, "Hello, are you John
Hancock?"

"I better be," quipped John, "I'm wearin' his underwear."

"Well," she continued, "I'm a great fan of yours. I listen

every day. I know your dad's been ill. Is he still with you?"

"Yes, ma'am, my father will always be with me."

"Does he know how much you love him?"

"Well, I hope so," John replied. "I wrote him a long emotional letter once, just to make sure he knew what he meant to me. I think I wrote it more for myself than I did for him."

Further into the hour, the beat of Buddy Rich studded the air and John toasted, "This one's for you, Dad. Some of my fondest memories with my dad were when he taught me how to be a drummer—like learning how to do a double paradiddle."

A husky voice said, "Hey, Hancock, you've really opened a mind trap for me. I'm sitting here by the side of the road—blubbering and crying like a baby. I've never had much time for my dad. I put everything else first. I always meant to—but, well, you know. I just called him, telling him I'm pickin' up a bottle of Scotch and comin' over. He's hearin' your show today, too. I owe you one, buddy," and the voice choked off.

Each caller shared their lives and their fathers with the listening fans. Comments so beautifully expressed that it seemed as though they were reading from a planned script. Details of a hundredth birthday party; loving praise to a stepfather; kids from a family of six whose dad had raised them after Mom abruptly died. Stories heavy with sacrifice and dedication. Most of the time John merely listened, joining in only occasionally.

It was the last ten minutes of the show, when this caller said, "Hancock, I never miss your show, but I was a little late tuning in today—missed the first part. I know your dad had a stroke. Did your father pass away last week?"

John hesitated a second then responded, "No—he didn't."

"Well, you always seem to come up with the

unexpected. I hope you have some good news to tell us. My dad died years ago, but I see him every time I look in the mirror."

Then John said, "The clock tells me it's time to shut this show down but I need to share one more thing—about my dad. After midnight last night, my mom phoned with 'the call you don't ever want to get,' telling me my dad had just died."

All sound stopped on the station—dead air—an unpardonable sin in broadcasting. But in this case, excusable. It would later be reported that cars were spotted all over Charlotte, pulled to one side of the road—radio listeners sharing a few seconds of grief with John Hancock. He recovered his voice and struggled to continue. "After that call I found myself in a great state of denial. But my dad taught me to face up to things, to be a man's man. I didn't want to tell you ahead of time that he had died. It seemed only right for me to honor my father today by letting you pay tribute to yours. I'm one of the lucky ones. My grieving will be easier, I think, because my father and I found a sense of peace with each other that some people never find. After seven years on this air, my listeners have become like family. Family is what matters."

In the background, John began playing the hauntingly beautiful theme music from *On Golden Pond*, then spoke over the score of *Field of Dreams*. "I'll be gone for a few days to take my dad back home to Texas." By this time, John had quit trying to mask emotions or to stop the tears that clogged his voice. His words quivering, he choked, "Thanks for sharing your dads with me—and letting me share mine with you—on this thing we call 'radio.' This is John Hancock—out for now."

Ruth Hancock

The Nickel Story

*Life is eternal, and love is immortal, and death
is only a horizon, and a horizon is nothing save
the limits of our sight.*

Rossiter Worthington Raymond

"Hey, Red, you owe me a nickel!"

Susan had bumped Frank while he was playing pinball
in the bar where she waitressed. A red light flashed *TILT*
and the game was over. Reaching into her apron pocket,
Susan pulled out a nickel and flicked it to him, then went
back to her work.

"I'm going to marry her someday," Frank told the bar-
tender confidently.

"Sure you are!" he laughed. "She's been here a long time,
and I've never known her to even go out on a date. Good
luck!" Frank rubbed the nickel between his fingers, knowing it was his lucky charm.

Susan had made a life for herself as a young widow and
a single mother. The last thing she was thinking of was
complicating her life with a new man.

But Frank's lucky charm worked—Susan knocked his

socks off and stole Frank's heart on their first date. Soon he had not only won her heart, but her daughter's heart as well.

There were many hard times after their wedding. Frank was a military man who was shipped overseas, leaving Susan in the single-mother role once again. Another daughter kept her busy, and both daughters adored their daddy. The years passed by quickly.

Frank loved to tell the nickel story to anyone who would listen. His eyes sparkled as he spoke of his love for Susan. This was a man who truly loved his wife.

Their fiftieth wedding anniversary was a special day. Frank contacted me to do a floral arrangement for the church and a corsage for his bride. They renewed their vows on that Sunday morning following the worship service. Our band surprised them as they walked down the aisle by singing "their" song, "The Sunny Side of the Street." Their walk became a dance as Frank twirled Susan down the aisle. What a celebration! It was a joy to be in their presence.

Soon after this wonderful day, Frank got sick. He offered everyone a smile and continued to glow with his love of Susan. Frank was never one to complain. Having a strong faith, Frank knew he would be with the Lord soon. After a few long months of suffering, he died.

All the seats at the funeral home were taken as we gathered to honor the memory of this dear friend. We were all inspired by him in our own ways. The minister spoke of Frank with such love and respect. We laughed, and our hearts were warmed as he shared memories of this special man. And then he told the nickel story. He said that Frank had called him a week or so before he died and asked to see him. While they visited, Frank took out his lucky charm. He had held on to that nickel for all of these years.

"Frank told me to keep this for him," the minister said as

he reached into his pocket and walked over to Susan. "He wanted me to give it to you today and to tell you to hold onto it. He'll be waiting for you at the pinball machine."

Hana Haatainen Caye

Bubba's Secret Life

To touch the soul of another human being is to walk on holy ground.

Stephen R. Covey

The oldest of four children and the only girl, I often found myself frustrated with my three little brothers. As an adult, I see them in somewhat of a different light, but they will always be my *little* brothers.

We have always lived close to each other, and although we did not see one another every day, we kept in touch. My parents owned a grocery store, which my father ran, and we ran into one another at the store.

"Bubba," as I had nicknamed him when he was a baby, always came by the store before or after his shift. He was the oldest of my little brothers, and he was a deputy jailer at the county jail. To say that he was "laid-back" would be an understatement. His lack of attention to detail and tidiness often disturbed me. Being meticulous about my own house and property, I wondered how he could be so carefree and let things go. When he became a single parent, I worried he would not be able to "handle things." After a heartrending separation and divorce, he met a lovely woman and things were looking up. I expected an engagement announcement at any time.

One sunny afternoon last August, I got a phone call. The woman on the other end started by saying she was with the local county rescue squad. I paid little attention as I waited for her to ask if we could make a donation. She did not ask for money, but did ask if I had a brother named Bubba. I offhandedly answered, "Yes."

"Well, there's been an accident." There was a strange silence. I had been through this several times over the years. Bubba was hit head-on by someone who crossed the yellow line; his former wife had been in several rollover accidents.

Still undaunted, I asked, "Is he hurt? Did you have to take him to the hospital?"

When she did not answer, I guessed this was more serious. I asked again, "Is he hurt?"

This time she answered quietly, "Bubba didn't make it." The words echoed several times before they registered. What did she mean? "I'm so sorry . . ." I was numb, and her voice seemed to be fading away.

The next day, we met at the local funeral home to make the arrangements. It seemed like I was in the longest nightmare I had ever had. After picking out the casket and taking care of the family business, the pastor and Bubba's fellow deputies began asking about the service. Since Bubba was not a member of a church, we felt the logical choice would be the chapel in the funeral home. It would be more than adequate for our little family and a few friends. But the deputy felt the service should be held at the new middle school because law officers from all over the state often come in when a fellow officer is killed. I doubted that many of them even knew Bubba. After all, he was not a road deputy, but a jailer in a small county jail. I imagined how much worse we were going to feel in that large auditorium with just our little family and a few deputies. My parents agreed that whatever the deputies thought was best would be fine.

Visitation at the funeral home was the next night from seven until nine. We arrived early, so as not to miss anyone who might wander in. We entered through a rear door and could barely make our way through the crowd. I wondered who all of these people were and if they were the unfortunate friends and family of another deceased person. As we neared the chapel where Bubba was sleeping, as the children said, I could see there was already a long line of people waiting to file through. Outside, traffic in our little one-horse town was lined up for more than an hour. People filed in for more than two hours. *Who were these people?* I thought. Well, as it turned out, my brother had a "secret life."

He was a mechanic to those with car problems, a sitter for those with a baby in the hospital, a plumber to a desperate neighbor, a money lender, a lawn service, a moving company, a salvage man—each person came through the line with a story about how Bubba had been there for them in their time of need. No wonder he didn't have time to vacuum or take the trash out. He didn't have time to attend to those "important" details. He had "really important" business to take care of.

After the crowd had dwindled, we prepared to leave. As we were pulling out of the parking lot, I saw a sheriff's car pull in with three men in prison whites crowded in the back seat. This was one of my worst moments because I already knew what the funeral director would later confirm. These inmates had begged to say good-bye to their jailer. After the mortuary was locked up, they were brought in through the backdoor and stood, chained together, in front of the casket weeping. They took their cigarette and snack money and pooled it to buy flowers.

We were not alone in that big auditorium the next day—it was nearly full. Three pastor friends shared stories about their relationship with Bubba. Our youngest brother, Tracy, who has muscular dystrophy and has spent more than twenty years in a wheelchair, spoke. "People didn't think I would be able to do this, but my love for Bubba is stronger than my pain," he began. Tracy shared about his big brother; Gus shared about his partner; Joe shared about his friend; and Bubba's son T. J. shared about his daddy. Bubba had surely been all things to all people. In many ways we were uplifted, but inside I grieved all the more over the brother I never knew. I saw how many different losses he represented.

The procession, with nearly a mile of police cars with their blue lights flashing, was estimated to be four miles long. People stood along the highway with their hands over their hearts. Maybe it was a show of respect or maybe their hearts were aching like mine.

All of my life I thought I was doing all of the right things—keeping house, caring for my children, attending church and sending cards to the sick. I hadn't refused to help anyone, but I had not been out looking for the opportunity either. My priorities now seemed strangely ordered. Bubba's secret life taught me what was "really important."

Natalie "Paige" Kelly-Lunceford

My Son, a Gentle Giant, Dies

Bear with me this week, if you will, for a personal column.

It's about my son Christopher. He turned seventeen last November. He died on Thursday. He was a healthy, robust boy on Tuesday. He got sick on Wednesday. And he died on Thursday.

You would have liked him. Everyone did.

He was a gentle giant, everyone's best friend and the world's leading expert. On everything. He was always cheerful. He was, says the foreman at the farm where he worked this summer, simply "magical."

He was adopted. I say this with relish and love because adoption usually is mentioned only in stories about bad kids. In newspaper stories, serial murderers are adopted. Nobel Prize winners aren't. It's sort of a newspaper's code for saying, "Don't blame the parents. It's not their fault he killed the neighbors." But in this case, it's not my fault he was such a great kid.

So we looked not alike at all, and he thought that was funny. I'm 5'8" and weigh about 160. He was close to 6'4", I imagine, and weighed around 300. He looked like a cement block with a grin. Once, a year or so ago, he introduced me to a friend. "This is my dad," he said proudly. The friend looked at me, looked at Chris and then looked confused. "You should see my mother," Chris said with a straight face.

I mentioned him in a column here last November 29— that was his seventeenth birthday. I wrote about the death of Finnegan, our old floppy-eared hound, and I told how when Christopher was six he and I had taken a trip. I asked him about our two dogs, Finnegan and a clipped-ear Bouvier named Mandy. "Who do you like the best," I asked, "Finnegan or Mandy?"

"Finnegan," he quickly replied, "because his ears are so big you can wipe your tears on them."

He read the column that evening. "Did you get paid for writing that?" he asked. Yes, I did, I said. How much? he asked. I told him. "You know," he said, "that column wouldn't have been anything without that quote from me. I think I should get half."

That's the kind of kid he was. He always had an angle.

He was loving.

He loved everyone, especially his grandparents, but even his mom and dad. "I love you, Dad," he'd say with meaning and without embarrassment. He knew that was unusual. The summer before last, he and my wife and I played golf one Saturday—he could hit a golf ball a mile, though you never knew whether it would be a mile east or a mile west—and he asked what we were doing for dinner later. "Mom and I are going out," I said. "Do you want to go with us?"

"Nah," he said, "I think I'll do something with Joey." I pushed him to join us. Finally, he said, "Look, Dad, you don't understand. At my age you're not even supposed to *like* your parents."

He was funny.

"Dad," he said a couple of months ago, "I know what I'd

like for my next birthday—a handicapped-parking sticker. You know, there are a lot more places than there are people who use them." I explained that it was unlikely that they'd give a robust kid a handicapped-parking sticker. So Christopher, who didn't much care for studying, changed his tack: "You know, if I had one I could leave for everywhere I go ten minutes later—and I could use that time for studying."

As a parent, you live in fear your child will die in a car wreck, and in his year and a half of driving Christopher did manage to wreck all four of our family cars. He hit a tree the day he got his license. ("It wasn't my fault, Dad." "Well, Christopher," I said, "it was yours or the tree's." He knew that, he said, and then argued, almost persuasively, how the tree was to blame.) And last spring he backed one of my cars into another of my cars, which must be a record of sorts. He announced his other accident to me over the phone by beginning, "Dad, you know those air bags stink when they go off."

But it was a sudden, initial attack of juvenile diabetes that killed him, despite medical heroics and fervid prayers. It is awful and horrible and sad, and no words can comfort his four grandparents, his brother and sister, his friends or his parents.

Yet his friend Tim Russert of NBC called Friday, devastated as we all are, and said the only thing that has helped.

"If God had come to you seventeen years ago and said, 'I'll make you a bargain. I'll give you a beautiful, wonderful, happy and healthy kid for seventeen years, and then I'll take him away,'" Tim said, "you would have made that deal in a second."

And that was the deal.

We just didn't know the terms.

Michael Gartner

Going On

My best friend, James, lived on the farm next to ours just outside a small town in Ohio. My father was the town doctor. Jim's father was a farmer who could make anything he planted grow. My father kept a few head of cattle and some horses. The only thing we grew was fodder for our animals. So while Jim had to work a lot on his dad's farm, I could get my chores done in a couple of hours.

After school we often walked the two-plus miles to his house. There was, on that country road, a bridge that spanned Twelve Mile Creek. The roadbed was about fifteen feet above the water and, in the spring when the rains made the water deep enough, we used to get naked and jump off the bridge a time or two on our way home.

It was a scary and, we thought, daring thing to do. There was also a sign that said diving from the bridge was forbidden, but it didn't say anything about jumping so we believed we were on the right side of the law. There were plenty of boys in our school who wouldn't do it, and that fact made us feel heroic.

After our jumps, we would sit on a rock in the sun until we were dry enough to put on our clothes. Those were the times we would really talk about stuff. Jim wanted to be a farmer like his father and his grandfather. He had the gift for it and the will to do it. I wanted to find a way out of my hometown. I wanted to see how people lived all over the world, to know how they did things, how they thought.

Unlike almost everyone else who had a goal closer to home, Jim did not discourage me or tell me that I ought to want what he wanted like lots of people do. If they farm they want you to be a farmer, or if they have a business they think you should have one, too.

Jim was easy about the plain fact that life would part us, that we would grow up into men who would not see each other every single day. Strangely, this was the part of my future I did not want to come about. Even though I was determined to leave town, I was also determined not to leave my friend. That made an interesting dilemma that we talked about now and then.

"Well, Bud," he said one day, "there's this about life. You can't have something both ways. That's just a fact."

"I know that," I said, "but because something is a fact doesn't stop me from wanting it not to be."

He laughed then. He had a huge laugh for such a little guy. I was about six inches taller than he was, and he was about six inches smarter than me . . . he liked to say that.

"Well, good luck," he said. Then, "Let's do one more. I feel like one more."

And he got up from the rock, ran to the bridge, climbed up on the guardrail and balanced for a moment. The bright sun shone on him and made him look radiant. Then, instead of jumping, he dove.

He pushed off hard from the edge of the bridge, arched his back and spread his arms in one of the best swan dives I had ever seen. He seemed to hover in the air before he ducked his head, straightened his body and cut into the water.

We went home after that to his house. His mother was

the best baker who ever lived, according to me. She made bread every other day so her kitchen always had that yeasty smell I loved. And in the spring she made nutmeg cookies . . . big, round, rich, white cookies that made milk taste better than you could ever imagine. And that is what we had that day, sitting in the kitchen talking to Jim's mother as she worked. It seemed to me she knew almost everything, including the capital of Paraguay! It was no wonder to me that Jim loved her so much.

The next day Jim was not in school, and I thought his dad had kept him home to work on the farm because spring was a heavy-duty time for a farm family. But when he didn't appear the day after that, I got worried. I was about to call him up when my dad called me at home and said he was coming to pick me up. That scared the daylights out of me.

Though I sometimes went on calls with him after school, I was always the one to initiate that adventure. He never called me to go with him. When I asked him why on the phone, he said he'd be home in a minute. And he was.

As we drove the short distance from our house, he told me that Jim was sick. He had a virulent pneumonia, and there was nothing anyone could do except wait and pray.

When we got to the farmhouse, Jim's dad opened the door, and I followed my father into the house and up to the second floor. There was only one light in the room, and it was beside the bed where Jim was lying, covered with blankets and breathing hard. His mother stood beside the bed and was in the act of changing a compress on his head when we arrived.

I was more frightened than I had ever been in my life. My father examined my friend, and then he bent over his body and began to breathe into his mouth. He did that for a very long time, until there was a sudden rasp of air from Jim's lungs. Then silence. My dad kept on breathing for him until Jim's mother went to the other side of the bed and put her hand on my father's shoulder.

"He's gone, Doc," she said, and sat down on the bed next to her son. Jim's father led us out of the room, and I followed my father to the car to make the long, terrible drive home.

I did not know what to do. I did not know how to get hold of my feelings. I spent most of the time crying and the rest of the time trying not to cry. Jim's family had his funeral from their house as many people did in that small town. Everyone came. Everyone went to the cemetery. Everyone looked awful.

For weeks afterwards, I moped through my life. My mother and father tried to help me, to talk to me, but I heard nothing. I went to school still, but didn't work or speak much to anyone. I just shut everyone out. Everyone.

Then on a Friday, as summer neared, I walked the gravel road that led to the bridge where I had last been with my friend. As I came closer, I was astonished to see someone sitting on our rock. I shielded my eyes against the sun and could tell immediately it was Jim's mother.

She saw me coming and motioned to me to sit beside her. I really didn't want to do that, but I understood I had to. We sat for a long time, not saying anything at all. I felt worn out and so sad that I couldn't speak. Finally, I leaned my head against her shoulder. She put her arm around me, and I just lost it.

She said nothing while I wept the last of my tears. Her dress smelled of her kitchen, and somehow that comforted me a little. Finally, when I could speak, I said, "I can't get over it. I just can't."

"Why would you want to?" she said in a soft, sweet voice.

"That's what you have to do," I said. "'Get over it, get

past it, move on,' people said."

"You just told me you can't do that. And you are right. What we have to do is make Jim's dying a part of us, just as the rest of his life was. You must take it into yourself. Breathe it in. Take it into your soul and let it remake you. A young man who has lost his best friend is a very different young man from one who has never had such a thing happen."

What she said struck me with such clarity that I sighed and sat up. Sunlight dazzled the surface of the water below us. And for the first time in many days, I could once again see my friend . . . see how he had helped shape my life and how he would be a part of it forever.

We sat together for a long time. Then Jim's mother patted my hand and said, "Cookies?" And so we walked in the fullness of the day, between the hedgerows and Queen Anne's lace, past the fields of corn growing, ever growing, to the farmhouse on the hill where I had learned so much about love.

Walker Meade

Opening Day in Heaven

Opening Day—two words that conjure up memories of seasons long past and of lazy days passed by fathers and sons at ballparks all over America. It's a marvelous, cathartic day, when everyone is young again, spring is in the air, and everything is fresh and new.

I'm not sure Opening Day will ever be the same for me again.

Last September, my wife and I stared in disbelief as doctors told us that our son Mikey was suffering from a rare form of brain cancer called pontine glioma and had a few short weeks to live.

It couldn't happen to him. He was so healthy, strong and full of life; it had to be something else that was causing his sudden awkwardness and loss of balance. There was no chance that a normal kid could have no symptoms one day and be terminal the next.

In just five short weeks, we found out we were wrong. Our five-year-old son died on October 16, 1999.

At the time of his death, baseball was just starting to have some significance in his life, and the memory of his last game has forever changed my perspective on the sport I fell in love with more than thirty-five years ago.

Mikey had seen the Yankees when they came to town, and Mark McGwire, too, but it was the Phillie Phanatic mascot that held his fascination.

He listened to me retell countless stories of my late father seeing Babe Ruth and Lou Gehrig in the 1920s and the time he introduced me to Mickey Mantle for my tenth birthday. I told him about a magical October night when Reggie Jackson blasted three pitches out of Yankee Stadium in game six of the 1977 World Series. But Mikey really wanted to meet the Phanatic.

A local bank arranged for our family to be their guest in the firm's luxury box for the last game of the season. I contacted the Philadelphia Phillies, and within an hour Mikey had a date with the chubby green mascot.

In the fifth inning of a meaningless game, Mikey got his wish.

The visit lasted only a few minutes, but he was as excited and animated as I've ever seen him. I couldn't help but think that I must have had the same look on my face when I met Mickey Mantle.

For a few minutes, we almost forgot what inevitably lay ahead.

We settled back down to watch the rest of the game. After innumerable sodas and soft pretzels, I took the lad to the men's room. As I helped him tuck in his shirt, he said to me in a world-weary voice, "Dad, this is my last game."

"Don't say that, Mikey," I replied. "There will be plenty of other games. You'll see."

"No, Dad . . ." his voice trailed off. Then suddenly, young again, "Is there baseball in heaven?"

"Of course there is, pal," I said as I tried to keep my composure. "And all the great players are there. It must be something to see."

"Do you think Grandpop will take me to a game?" he asked.

Forgive me today if I skip the box scores in tomorrow's edition—because the game I'm interested in won't get much coverage. It's Opening Day in heaven.

I hope the Babe and Mickey hit a couple of home runs for the little boy with the big hot pretzel sitting in the box seats next to my father.

Mike Bergen

Never Good at Good-Bye

Those who loved you and were helped by you will remember you. So carve your name on hearts and not on marble.

C. H. Spurgeon

"Paper or plastic?"

It was a familiar voice I heard at least once a week. His name was Frank, and he bagged groceries for a living in our small one-grocery-store town in rural South Carolina. He was rarely seen without his baseball cap and that crooked smile he wore from ear to ear.

"Plastic is fine."

That was just the beginning of our conversation during my weekly visits. He, at his own speed, loaded all my groceries in white plastic bags as I waited patiently to follow him out the door. I was very aware of the limp he tried so hard to hide. He was in his late twenties and mildly retarded. During our conversations, he would repeat himself, then laugh. We went to the same church, but when we saw each other there, I never said much more than hello. It was during my trips to the grocery store where we shared the most time.

I was amazed at the social calendar Frank kept. I knew he was always faithful to our church; there was never a time he wasn't there. He told me of trips to the local YMCA and baseball games he wouldn't miss. Once all my groceries were in the car, he would linger in the parking lot until finally he would give me a bear hug that almost knocked me down! Frank never was good at good-bye. I'd kiss him on the cheek and promise to see him on Sunday.

One hot, summer morning, I made my weekly trip to the grocery store, but as soon as I walked into the building, I could sense something terribly wrong. Instead of the morning "hellos" and cheerful clerks, all I saw were heads hung low and many crying. I immediately looked for Frank, knowing he would tell me what was going on. I didn't see him bagging groceries, so I assumed he was stocking the shelves. I went down every aisle looking for him. As I stood at the last aisle, my heart beat fast and my throat tightened. I quietly walked to a small office in the back, and I saw an older man with his head down on his desk, weeping. I put my hand on his back to comfort him, and in between his sobs, I heard a shrill, "Oh, Frank!"

My dear friend Frank had drowned on a fishing trip. My heart had never experienced such sadness. I wanted to tell the world how this young man had lifted my spirits on so many rainy days.

On the afternoon of his funeral, I went to support his family even though we had never met. I didn't expect many people to be there because Frank was a simple man. As I pulled into the parking lot of my church, I was stunned because I could barely find a parking spot.

Once I walked into the church, I got the last seat in the last row. I heard ushers behind me telling other anxious people there was an overflow section in another part of the building. It was very obvious people around me were thinking the same thing. *Why were there so many here for Frank's funeral? It's as if we are burying a famous person or political leader.* Half an hour later than the funeral was scheduled to begin, and after everyone was finally seated, the pastor rolled up his sleeves and slowly walked up to the pulpit. He stood there, silently, as if trying to gain his composure. Tears fell down his face, and just as he was about to speak, someone two rows up stood. He was a tall, burly man; he must have stood over six feet tall.

"I would just like to say, Frank came into my store three days a week with a bucket and some soap. He cleaned my bathrooms until they shined, and he would never take a red cent. I won't forget him." He sat down, not trying to hide the tears.

And then someone else rose. It was an elderly lady who stood with a cane.

"Every time I went to the grocery store, Frank would put this little paper into my bag." Out of her purse she pulled a little tattered card. "It always said thank you for being so kind."

A young boy, not much taller than the pew he stood in front of, proudly said, "Frank went to every one of my baseball games whether I played or not."

Story after story was repeated that day. The funeral lasted more than four hours, and many people still lingered, waiting to honor the memory of such a remarkable man. Frank's family had no idea of the life he had led; he was just a "good son," his mother and father said. Many of us there that day were changed forever.

Frank never was good at good-bye, but that day he outdid himself.

Amanda Dodson

5

SPECIAL MOMENTS

Each one of us is born for a specific reason and purpose, and each one of us will die when he or she has accomplished whatever was to be accomplished. The in-between depends on our own willingness to make the best of every day, of every moment, of every opportunity. The choice is always yours.

Elisabeth Kübler-Ross

Trailing Clouds of Glory

Death has many secrets, and I know few or none of them. However, I've been given a story to tell—a story about a time when that thick veil of mystery tore open just a little bit and then closed up again.

One glimpse that ignited a lifetime of faith.

It happened about a month after my thirtieth birthday. The school year had ended, and I was finishing up final grade reports for my students. The house was a mess, and my suitcase was half-packed. In two days, I would fly to California. My father had been sick for months, and his voice over the phone had been sounding weaker and weaker. Good thing I'd be seeing him soon, wrapping things up. Nice and tidy.

Then that night, some time before dawn, without moving a finger or twitching an eyelid, I suddenly rose up out of a deep sleep, like a boulder floating to the surface of the sea. I didn't wake up in the usual sense. That is, I was wakeful but not awake. It's hard to explain. I simply found myself . . . somewhere. Talking with someone. Someone big and wonderful. I didn't know who, and I didn't think how. I really didn't think at all. I just felt warmth and love, and safety and peace. I couldn't see much, just a shape, a shadowy figure. But I heard a voice, a big voice. *Hello,* it said, *I've missed you. I love you.*

The encounter lasted several minutes, and the emotions are still vivid to this day. Like a lion cub getting licked with affection, I was floating in bliss.

Then I slipped back into slumber. When I awoke in the morning sunlight, I remembered the pre-dawn visitation clearly. I had overslept. The alarm hadn't sounded—my electric clock had stopped.

The very moment of mechanical failure was obvious to see: a quarter to three. The hands had locked in their tracks, flung open as though ready for a hug at the nine and the three.

About an hour later, the phone call came. It was my mother. My dad had died early that morning.

The news hit me like an explosion. After the initial shock, I realized what had happened while I slept. I turned to look at the clock again. It had stopped at the exact moment my dad had died.

My father had stopped to visit me on his way out of this dimension.

For the first time in my life, I experienced what the Hawaiians call *He ho'ike na ka po*—a revelation of the night. They believe that dreams can be a bridge between this world and the next.

In the context of ordinary dreams, I'd always considered the notion to be sentimental and vague.

But what I experienced was no ordinary dream. The meeting was vivid and clear, and my dad's message was so reassuring that I am moved to share it: *I'm happy,* he said in a wordless voice. *What a relief to be released from that body . . . to range so freely . . . to grow so wide. I can't say much, there's only a moment to check in, but—wow. Would you just look at me?*

And I couldn't look at him because my eyes were not

capable of zeroing in on the heavenly realms that he now inhabited.

I didn't worry about my dad after that. I knew he was experiencing something about death, something big. And he'd made a point to stop by and share some of it with me. In fact, for a moment he pulled me along.

As I am writing this, I stop to read again those famous lines from Wordsworth's *Intimations of Immortality*:

> *Not in entire forgetfulness and not in utter nakedness,*
> *but trailing clouds of glory do we come from God, who*
> *is our home.*

When my dad sailed past, I got caught up in the clouds of glory that he was trailing, and I got to peek through that doorway. What I saw and felt is not something that I can articulate. But I began to see that the mysteries of life and death amount to so much more than I had ever imagined.

I kept that little electric clock in my closet. Then, five years later, someone tried to get the clock to work again.

I had hired a housecleaner, and she went at her job with a voracious ambition. She vacuumed the box springs of the bed and sanded the toilet seat so I wouldn't slip off in the middle of the night. She got into my closet, ironed my socks and re-laced all my shoes. Then she found the clock.

When I got home that night, I saw the ironed socks and the textured toilet seat. Then I saw my father's parting memento. The cheap little plastic clock was sitting under the bed where she had plugged it in, trying to get it to work. She had tried resetting the clock so it no longer said quarter to three. It no longer said anything meaningful. And it still didn't work. Now, instead of a sacred relic, the clock was just a piece of junk.

I made a mental note to throw it away, but then I forgot about it.

Three days later, I remembered and looked under the bed again.

There was the clock. Somehow, it had re-set itself to the time it wanted to proclaim: a quarter to three.

My eyebrows went up in astonishment. My brain was trying to explain what I was experiencing, but it couldn't. So then I simply unplugged the clock, carried it to my office and set it on the shelf over my desk where it sits today.

Whenever I see it, I remember.

And that's all I have to say on the subject of death.

Paul D. Wood

THE FAMILY CIRCUS. By Bil Keane

"Grandma says it's okay that this life
won't last forever—the next one will."

Reprinted with permission from Bil Keane.

The Beach Trip

It wasn't a typical trip to Carolina Beach. Oh, I had the cooler, beach chair and towel, but it still wasn't the same. I wasn't going to the beach to relax—I was going to remember my son, Cameron, who died of leukemia in March 1998. You see, on this day Cameron would have turned twenty-one.

I decided to go to a favorite part of Carolina Beach—the one within walking distance of a McDonald's (in case you get bored of the beach and want some fries).

Now, it's typical that little kids are drawn to me. Maybe it's the fact that I smile at them, maybe it's the fries, but it does happen. So I was not surprised to have one small child covering my feet with sand and another playing with his toys right by my beach chair. Their parents were seated behind me, and the two boys spent about an hour running back and forth from my chair to their parents'.

"What's your name?" I asked the oldest.

"Alex. I'm five."

"Oh, I have a son named Alex. He's twelve."

He continued covering my feet with sand until his parents walked by on their way to the water's edge.

"I'm going in with my parents."

"Okay."

"My little brother HATES the water—he doesn't go in ever."

"That's okay. I'll watch him while you go into the ocean with your mom and dad."

The smallest boy, about one-and-a-half, watched his brother run off, turned to me and reached up. Of course I picked him up, sat him on my lap and offered him some fries. We waved to the family down in the water, ate chips and just chilled out.

Suddenly, he slipped off my lap, took my hand and pulled me toward the water. I walked him to the edge, and he giggled when the water lapped over his feet. When a bigger wave came and hit his legs even harder, he started laughing. I scooped him up, swung him around, put him on my hip and walked over to his mom and dad.

"What a cutie he is," I said.

"Oh, he's very afraid of the water. I can't believe he's in the water at all."

I told them that he had taken my hand and pulled me in. "I told your son Alex that I have a son named Alex at home. Your little one is so cute. What's his name?"

"Cameron."

And my heart stopped. I looked into that little boy's eyes, and he looked right back and touched my face.

Thank you, Cameron.

Dawn Holt

I Still Choose "Mom"

I watched through blurred vision as my husband, Chuck, walked away with his ex-wife.

The heaviness in all our hearts was almost unbearable. Turning back to my stepson's casket I somehow helped my children pluck a rose from the brother spray to press in their Bibles. With tears streaming down my face, I rested my hand on the son spray. I no longer knew my place.

God, I silently screamed, *how did I fit in Conan's life?*

From the moment I'd met my stepson, I was in awe of this angelic little boy whose bright, blond hair seemed to glow with a heavenly radiance. At only a year-and-a-half, he was built like a three-year-old. Solid and stocky, sleeping curled in my lap, his tiny heart beat against mine, and a maternal bonding began stirring inside me.

Within a year I became a stepmother to Conan and his older sister, Lori. Soon after that, a visit to the doctor revealed some disheartening news.

"You have an infertility disease," the doctor had said. "You might not ever have children of your own."

At twenty-two, that news was shattering. I had always wanted to be a mother. Suddenly, I realized being a stepmother might be as close as I would get, and I became even more involved in their lives.

But thankfully, four years later we joyfully discovered I was pregnant. Chase was born, then two years later we were blessed with our daughter, Chelsea.

I loved being both a mom and a stepmother, but as in any blended family, it had its ups and downs. Chuck's ex-wife had custody of his kids and gave them more freedom than we gave our children. Needing to be consistent with our rules, I'm certain we appeared overly strict to his kids. On their weekend visitations, I usually felt like an old nag.

As a second wife, I was jealous of my stepchildren's mother. I complained about her and her husband within earshot of my stepkids, and even grumbled about buying my stepchildren extras on top of paying child support. Somehow I overlooked the important fact that my step-children were the innocent ones thrust into a blended family.

Then one day at a gathering of my own family, I watched as my mother went up to my stepmother and gave her a hug. I turned and saw my father and stepfather laughing together. Having always appreciated the cooperative relationship my parents and stepparents had, it occurred to me that Chuck's children longed for the same. So Chuck and I decided to work hard at bridging gaps instead of creating them.

It wasn't easy, and changes didn't come overnight, but they did come. By the time Conan was fifteen, a peace had settled between parents and stepparents. Instead of griping about child-support payments, we voluntarily increased them. And finally Conan's mom gave us copies of his report cards and football schedules.

I was proud of my kids and stepkids. After graduation, my stepdaughter married, and she and her husband built a house together. At seventeen, Conan had become a sensible, intelligent young man. With rugged good looks and a deep, baritone voice, I wondered what fortunate girl would snatch him up.

But then came that phone call, changing our lives forever—Conan was killed instantly by a drunk driver.

Over the years we'd been married, Chuck had reassured me that I was a parent to his children, too. He sought my opinion in matters concerning them and relied on me to make their Christmases and birthdays special. I enjoyed doing those things and looked upon myself as their second mother.

But in his grief immediately upon Conan's death, Chuck suddenly stopped seeking my opinion and began turning to his ex-wife. I knew they had to make many final decisions together, and I realized later that he was trying to spare me from the gruesom details, but for the first time, I began to feel like an outsider instead of a parent.

I also knew the driver responsible for the accident had to be prosecuted, which meant Chuck and his ex-wife would have to stay in contact. Those ugly jealousies from the past began to resurface when, night after night, he talked to her, seldom discussing their conversations with me.

And it stung when friends inquired only about Chuck's coping, or sent sympathy cards addressed just to him, forgetting about me and even our two children. Some belittled my grieving because I was "just" a stepparent. Did anyone realize my loss and pain? I'd had strong maternal feelings for Conan; he considered me his second mother— or did he? As the weeks turned into months, that question haunted me, dominating my thoughts. I became driven to understand just what my role had been.

I rummaged through boxes of photos and dug out old journals, searching the house for mementos, even Christmas ornaments he had made.

There were several comforting journal excerpts, one

describing Mother's Day phone calls from Conan to me, and a beautiful white poinsettia he gave me at Christmas. And I cherished the memories old photos brought back—his loving bear hugs after cooking his favorite meal—or a kiss for simply doing his laundry. As comforting as these things were, they still weren't enough.

One beautiful spring day, almost a year after he died, I was lovingly caressing the pressed rose from his grave that I kept in my Bible. Suddenly, I felt compelled to visit his grave alone. I had never done that before, but I desperately needed some answers.

Arriving at the gravesite, I remembered Chuck mentioning that the permanent headstone had recently arrived. Chuck had told Conan's mom to select what she wanted. As I looked down on the shiny marble surface, I noticed she had chosen a bronze sports emblem, along with a picture of Conan that had been permanently embedded under a thick layer of glass.

I bent down and lovingly ran my fingers over his engraved name and the dates commemorating his short life. Through a mist of tears, memories of a rambunctious, fun-loving little boy filled my heart. The child I'd mothered part-time for so many years may not have come through my body, but I had been chosen by God to provide a maternal influence in his life. Not to take his mother's place, but to be just a "step" away. I suddenly felt very honored to have been chosen.

"It was a privilege to be your stepmother," I whispered out loud, bending to kiss his picture.

Finally, a sense of peace was beginning. With a heavy sigh, I got up to leave. But as I turned to walk away, the sun glistened on the border of the headstone, causing me to look back.

"Oh my gosh! How could I have not noticed it before?" The entire border of the headstone was trimmed in gold shafts of wheat . . . exactly like a gold shaft-of-wheat pin Conan had given me years ago. Chills ran up and down my spine. I hadn't seen that pin in years.

Somehow, I just knew it was the missing link. I *had* to find that pin.

The ride home was a blur. I was so excited. Finally, I was upstairs in my bedroom tearing apart my jewelry box. Where was it? Dumping the contents on the bed, I frantically tossed earrings and pins to and fro.

Nothing.

God, this is important. Please help me find it, I prayed.

Turning from the bed I felt compelled to search my dresser. Rummaging through drawer after drawer proved futile, until finally, in the last drawer, clear in the back I felt it. It was a small, white box with my name scribbled on top in a child's handwriting. Prying it open, I was instantly transported back in time.

Conan had been about ten years old, and it was the night before going on vacation to Florida. He was going with us, and I was packing in my room when I heard a knock on my door. Conan stood there, his eyes downcast and his hands behind his back.

"What is it, son?" I asked, concerned by this unexpected visit.

Shuffling his feet, he quickly mumbled, "I don't know why I don't call you 'Mom' very often, even though I call my stepdad 'Dad.'"

I hugged him and reassured him he was free to call me whatever he was comfortable with. Then suddenly, with a wry smile on his pudgy face, he handed me the small, white box.

"You choose," he said, and darted from the room.

Assuming I'd find two items inside the box, I opened it. Instead, I found the single gold wheat pin he'd bought at a garage sale with his own money.

Scribbled inside the lid of the box were the words, "I Love You. To Mom or Connie."

That had been almost a decade ago, yet as I pushed the spilled contents of my jewelry box aside and slowly sat down on the edge of the bed, it felt like yesterday.

Thank you, God, for finding this pin, and for the closure that comes with it.

Wiping the tears from my face, I reflected on an angelic little boy whose heart beat close to mine.

I still choose "Mom."

Connie Sturm Cameron

Ballerina

My father was a tall, ruggedly handsome man with raven hair and gentle brown eyes. His name was Bernard, and he was an avid sport fisherman. He used to take my brothers and me fishing from a rowboat on a lake, or from the shore of a gently flowing stream. He ran a tackle shop in the middle of Manhattan. The store was never terribly successful, so to help make ends meet, my father sold the exquisite paintings he created without the benefit of a single day of formal training.

How vividly I still recall the endless happy hours I spent as a little girl in my father's tiny studio watching him put brush to canvas. *It's like magic,* I thought of the way he could turn dollops of color into striking portraits, still lifes or seascapes.

One of my very favorites was a ballet scene a family friend commissioned my father to paint for his wife's anniversary gift. For years the painting hung prominently in the living room of their elegant New York home. Every time we went for a visit I'd stand mesmerized by its beauty, half-convinced that any moment the graceful dancers would spring to life before my very eyes. Eventually, the couple moved away, and our families lost touch. But over the years that painting has always kept a very special place in my heart.

My father never had much money, but he did without so he could buy me the prettiest dresses or take me out for ice-cream sodas on sultry summer afternoons. He held me sobbing in his arms the day my puppy died and brought me special treats when I was sick in bed with the flu.

I felt so beautiful my wedding day when I walked down the aisle on my father's arm. He became a doting grandpa to my three children, Tracy, Binnie and David. Once, when three-year-old Tracy drew him a picture, Dad put it in his wallet and said he'd carry it with him always. "That boy is going to become a real artist; you just wait and see," he predicted.

I was only thirty when my father died. I felt so alone and adrift. "I'm not ready to let him go," I sobbed to my mom the night of his funeral.

I missed my father terribly. There was so much I longed to share with him. How proud he would have been when I returned to school and became an English teacher after my kids were grown. He would have swelled with pride when David became a dentist, when Binnie published her first children's book, and most especially when Tracy fulfilled his grandpa's prediction and became a successful artist.

"Your father is still very much with you," my friends and family kept telling me. "He's watching over you from heaven." More than anything, I wished I could have believed them. But over the years I'd never once felt my father's presence.

"He's gone," I'd whisper sadly, poring through the family photo albums. "All I have left of Dad are a lot of happy memories."

Then tragedy struck. Pelvic pain sent me to the doctor, and the tests came back positive for ovarian cancer. The diagnosis felt like a death sentence.

Surgeons removed most of my cancer, but they couldn't get it all. "You'll need several months of chemotherapy, and even then I can't make any promises," the oncologist explained honestly.

My family embraced me with their love and support. "We'll get through this together," my husband, Barney, assured me. The chemo was so strong. A substitute teacher had to finish out my school year and begin the fall term while I lay flat on my back for weeks at a stretch. I was so frail, I couldn't stumble to the bathroom without struggling not to pass out.

Maybe I'd be better off throwing myself in front of a moving car, I thought more than once as I left the hospital after yet another infusion of toxic chemicals. How I yearned for those days long gone when I could curl up in my father's strong arms and feel safe and protected from any danger. Somehow, I survived the chemo. But I couldn't sleep at night, worrying if I'd also survived the cancer. A few weeks before Thanksgiving I went for a CAT scan. Then I returned home and anxiously awaited the results. The day before I was to learn whether I would live or die, I received a phone call from my brother Robert. "You'll never believe what happened to me today," he began, and by the time he'd completed his miraculous tale, tears of joy were spilling down my cheeks.

Every Sunday Robert visits an open-air antique market in Greenwich Village, hoping to add to his collection of cruise-ship memorabilia. "You were so much in my thoughts today," he told me over the phone. "I was praying for you, but I kept wishing there was something more I could do." Then, from several dozen yards away, Robert spotted a painting that was instantly familiar, despite the more than fifty years that had elapsed since he'd last seen it hanging from our friend's living-room wall. "I didn't even have to read the signature to know it was Dad's ballerina painting," my brother told me. "I've always remembered how much you loved it. I bought it on the spot, and I couldn't wait to get home and call you with the news." As Robert spun his tale, a radiant warmth filled my soul.

And then for the very first time since he died, I felt my father's presence. "Oh, Dad!" I thrilled. "You really have been watching over me from heaven, and now you've come back to be my guardian angel!" After I hung up the phone I gave Barney a jubilant hug.

"It's no coincidence Robert found that painting today," I wept happy tears. "My father knew how much I needed him, and he found a very special way to let me know everything's going to be just fine. My cancer is really gone."

The next morning I telephoned for the test results, but I already knew the answer. "You don't sound at all surprised," the doctor said after informing me I was completely cancer-free.

"My guardian angel already told me," I explained happily. These days, whenever I gaze upon my father's beautiful painting, I think about how much I loved my dad and remember all the times over the years when I longed for him to be there to share in my joy or my sorrow. But my father never really left me. I know that now. He's been with me through all my days, and he watches over me still, loving me and protecting me from harm just like long ago when I was a little girl.

Ferne Kirshenbaum
As told to Bill Holton

Mom's Stained-Glass Window

Without faith, we are as stained-glass windows in the dark.

Anonymous

Pat Lewis drove slowly down the country lane that led to Willow Heights County Home. The beauty of the New Jersey countryside—trees ablaze with color, mashed-potato clouds in a blue sky, winding little streams sparkling in the bright sunshine—cut into her heart. *This was the kind of day that Mom would have loved.* Pat's mind drifted back over the past few years.

She'd not expected to miss her mom so much. She'd always thought those lunches out, appointments with the hairdresser, impromptu shopping excursions or even grocery shopping trips were mainly for her mom's benefit. But over the past years, Pat had come to enjoy and even look forward to those times.

Her mom hadn't made any lasting friendships while she was married. Then, widowed ten years, she found herself lonely and alone, except for her daughter Pat, son-in-law Tom, grandchildren and great-grandchildren, who lived in faraway places. Living in Willow Heights County Home, she was surrounded by ladies in the same situation. Somehow, this did not draw her to any of them. Even though Willow Heights offered a planned schedule of social activities, Mom preferred to sit in her tiny living room and crochet.

Pat's parents had both immigrated as toddlers from Germany to America with their parents. Her mom had been a typical German *hausfrau*. She had cleaned, cooked, washed and ironed, scrubbed floors, baked bread and shined shoes, raised two children, and been grateful that she had been given the opportunity to do so. She'd lived in the same little, white-frame house all her married life. Every Sunday they attended the German Lutheran Church, only two blocks away.

Perhaps attending those services spurred her desire for a stained-glass window. She never really asked for anything, but once in a while she contemplated out loud how nice a small stained-glass window would look in the front door, the top part of the big living-room window or even the small window above the kitchen sink where the morning sun streamed through. No one ever took her desire seriously. Actually, it became a kind of family joke.

When Christmas drew near, or it was her birthday, someone would be sure to laugh and say, "Why don't we get Mom a stained-glass window?"

Through it all, her ninety-year-old fingers kept twisting and working her crochet hook, turning out jackets, coats and afghans. The afghans were the first to confuse her. They were too big to hold in her lap, and three-quarters of the way through, she could not remember the pattern. She crocheted three coats in a herringbone pattern. The last one, in shades of blue, had one arm finished in variegated colors simply because she had run out of the color she was using. Pat had unraveled it, and her mom immediately started to crochet pieces ranging in size from pot holders to pillowcases. Whenever she decided it was the right size, she simply edged it in a three-looped fan-shaped border and called it finished. Some of these strange little pieces were a good three inches wider at one end.

Emerald green, holly-berry red, deep violet, golden yellow and sapphire-blue skeins of yarn were quickly crocheted into ungainly squares.

Then, six months ago, Pat's mom suffered a massive heart attack and died in her sleep. Pat stuffed all the little pieces into a plastic trash bag and gave them to the supervisor, Mrs. Connelly, at Willow Heights. Perhaps a little splash of color under a flowerpot, or in some spot of the room of a resident, would add a note of cheer. Pat was just glad to get rid of the awkward pieces.

Pat pulled into the driveway of Willow Heights to attend the annual fall craft show featuring crafts made by the residents. She hadn't wanted to go, but Mrs. Connelly had insisted. As Pat entered the cafeteria-turned-showroom, Mrs. Connelly took her by the arm.

"I'm so glad you came," she said excitedly. "This is our best show ever! We've done something this year we never did before."

"And what is that, Mrs. Connelly?" Pat asked politely.

"Just you wait and see," the supervisor said as she steered Pat to the far end of the room where a small crowd had gathered. They were admiring a large afghan displayed on the wall. Pat gasped in astonishment. It was her mom's little crocheted pieces all joined in a yellow chain-stitch and edged by a three-looped, fan-shaped border.

"We raffled it off," Mrs. Connelly went on. "It's the first time we've ever had anything big enough to do that."

Pat stared as if hypnotized at the beautiful afghan. She could visualize Mom in her recliner, crocheting the little, crooked squares.

"You know," Mrs. Connelly said quietly, "as the afghan took shape, it seemed to assume a definite personality. Almost everybody in the home worked on it."

Pat couldn't take her eyes from it. The yellow yarn was the color of autumn sunshine and made the brightly colored squares look like . . .

Mrs. Connelly's voice cut into Pat's thoughts. "They've already decided what they're going to do with the money," she said. "They want to put a little stained-glass window in the wall, right in back of the altar where they can all see it."

Pat's lips quivered, and her tearful eyes were riveted on the afghan.

Mrs. Connelly looked at Pat quizzically. "Pat," she said softly, "would that be okay? Do you think your mother would like that?"

"She'd just love it."

Katherine Von Ahnen

I Still See Him Everywhere

Let mourning stop when one's grief is fully expressed.

Confucius

[EDITORS' NOTE: *On February 22, 1983, young Todd Morsilli of Warwick, Rhode Island, was struck and killed by a drunk driver. He was one of 19,500 Americans who lost their lives that year in accidents caused by intoxicated drivers. One October, Todd's father was asked to speak to students at Riverdale Country School, just north of Manhattan, about teenage drunk driving. As he looked around the assembly hall, Richard Morsilli wondered what he could say to persuade the students to listen. They seemed bored and restless. He felt he couldn't lecture. All he really wanted to do was to tell them how much he missed Todd. Which, more or less, is what he did. His talk, interspersed with his thoughts as he addressed the teenagers, follows.*]

Good morning. My name is J. Richard Morsilli. Eight months ago my son Todd was struck and killed by a seventeen-year-old drunk driver. Todd was thirteen. He was a wonderful boy.

Why did I say he was wonderful? Every father thinks his kid is special. But Todd really was. He had a knack for making people feel good about themselves. The day before he was killed, I heard him say to Carole, "Hey, Mom, my friends think you're pretty."

Todd was a tennis player. He was ranked third in his age group in New England in singles, first in doubles. He was also a baseball player, and when he was younger that's all he cared about, even after we got a tennis court. Then one day his older brother had no one to play with and persuaded Todd to pick up a racket. In six months Todd was winning tournaments.

That's what made us so close, my driving him to tournaments and having all that time in the car together. *That fellow in the third row with the sun-bleached hair has the same thoughtful look Todd would get when we'd discuss things.*

It sounds like Todd was really competitive, but he wasn't. I'd say, "Todd, how will you play this guy? I hear he's got a terrific cross-court return." And he'd say, "Gee, Dad, I don't know. I haven't thought about it." He liked to win, but he didn't much like to beat people. His coach urged him to play older kids to sharpen his skills, but he hated to do it because he knew it upset them to get beaten by a youngster.

I was the one who had visions of Wimbledon. All Todd ever said was, "That's a long way off, Dad. A lot can happen." Did he sense what was coming, like the garden that blooms like crazy just before frost?

Last February twenty-second, Todd was walking along the street with his cousin Jeff. The two boys were only five weeks apart in age and inseparable. Jeff had been watching Todd play tennis that morning, and they were on their way to rent skis for a Catholic Youth Organization weekend. First they stopped at our house to get money for ice-cream cones. "You know, Mom," Todd said after she had given him what change she had in her pocketbook, "what we'd really like are milk shakes." His mother laughed and went upstairs for more money.

That girl in the third row with the sweet face just caught her breath. She's thinking what Carole can't help but think—that if she'd said no, the boys would have left the house earlier; they'd have turned the corner before the car came.

An elderly neighbor told us that he was shoveling his driveway when the boys went by. It was a holiday, Washington's birthday, and the sun sparkling on the snow made the world seem paved with diamonds. The boys offered to finish the job for him, but he said he was glad to be outside, and they went on. The neighbor saw the car coming. Jeff saw it, too. The car was weaving. They both shouted, and Jeff jumped into a snowbank, but Todd . . . Todd . . . couldn't get out of the way.

Oh, God, help me get through this without crying. I've got to keep going.

The car . . . struck Todd. He was . . . thrown ninety feet. . . . The car didn't stop. . . .

It's been eight months. Will I ever be able to talk about it without breaking down?

I'm sorry. Forgive me. You just can't imagine how . . . overwhelming it is. I got a call at my office. It was someone at the hospital. The voice said, "A boy's been hurt. We think it's your son. Can you come right away?" All I remember is saying, over and over: "Just let there be a chance. He'll make it if he has a chance, because he doesn't give up."

He didn't get his chance. At the hospital a priest met me and took me into a little room. . . . Todd's mother and I didn't even have time to hope. By the time we knew about it at all, he was gone.

He's gone, and I still see him everywhere. I see him as I glance around this hall. In the clean line of your chin, there on the aisle. And there, first row middle, in your slim, strong frame. And in you, too, young lady, in the way he bit his lip to keep the tears from coming.

The next thing you know you're preparing for a funeral. You're saying things like, "His grave's got to be under a tree." You're making telephone calls. You're answering the doorbell. His friends . . .

Little girls asking if they could have one of Todd's tennis shirts. Little boys intending just to shake hands, but then moving into my arms as though, if we hugged hard enough, we could blot out the emptiness.

Nine hundred people jammed the church for his funeral. "It was like he was everyone's best friend," a fifteen-year-old who spoke at the service said. "You were just glad he was your friend, too."

We buried Todd in his warm-up suit and cap. Everyone knew that beige felt cap. It was like the one worn by Frew McMillan, the South African tennis player. Todd admired him because he was always a gentleman on the court.

Afterward, we got letters from all over the country—hundreds of letters—from people who'd met Todd at tournaments. They pretty much said the same thing: We knew your son. He was a terrific tennis player. But, even more, he was such a nice boy.

Then the funeral was over. You've buried your son, and you go back to work. The world goes on. But things don't mean the same. I'm no different from your fathers. I wanted to provide a bright future for my family. All I can tell you now is I'd give up all I have in a minute if I could just have Todd back.

Shall I tell them about the fox? No, probably not. I don't want them to turn me off.

Because of Todd's tennis playing, there was a lot in the newspapers about the tragedy. They called it a hit-and-run accident, which it was, except that the girl ran into a tree a mile down the road so the police caught her right away. She'd spent the holiday drinking beer at a friend's house, starting at ten in the morning, and later they switched to vodka.

She goes to school. I see her at the supermarket. Is her life going on as usual? Did Todd's death make any difference?

People wanted to do something. They started a Todd Morsilli Memorial Fund. Somebody suggested renaming the tennis courts at Roger Williams Park in Providence in honor of Todd. In June the first annual Todd Morsilli Memorial Tournament was held there.

Sometimes I tell myself: He was just a thirteen-year-old boy. How could he have touched so many lives? Sometimes I think: It was just another tragedy. How could so many lives be so terribly changed by it? But it's true.

I worry about Todd's brother David. He looks so much like Todd that people expect him to be Todd. I worry about Todd's sister Lisa, because she and Todd were closest. I worry about Todd's kid sister Kristin. She was visiting a friend before the accident and hadn't seen Todd in two days. She's recently become very enthusiastic about tennis. Is she genuinely interested? Or is she trying to make up to us for Todd? And I worry about Jeff, Todd's cousin, because he lost his father four months before Todd was killed.

I pray every day he'll make it. I pray every day that all of us make it.

They say grief brings people closer together. It's not true—grief is isolating. It locks you up in your own heart. If Carole and I hadn't had such a good marriage, I think we'd have come apart. I was out of the house all day, but Carole was home, and everywhere she looked there was something to remind her of Todd. And I think the strain began to tell.

What saved us was the squirrel. If Kristin hadn't told Carole about the car in front of us hitting a squirrel and my getting out, pointlessly, to move the poor broken body to the side of the road and then sitting down on the curb sobbing, the silence might have won out over us. But that squirrel saved Carole and me. We talked to each other then. We realized we had to get help, and Carole took a part-time job to get out of the house.

I'm not on a crusade. As you know by now, I'm no speaker. And I didn't come to tell you not to drink. I only came to say that when you do drink, please, please call your parents to come get you. Because if something happens to you, it won't be just another tragedy; it'll be their beloved child. And if you kill someone else's child, it'll be someone like my son Todd. It doesn't have to happen. Don't let it happen.

I guess that's all I have to say. Thank you for listening.

Did I say enough? Did I say too much? Why, they're applauding. They're all standing up. That fellow is coming up on the platform. He's holding out his hand. They're lining up. Are they all going to shake my hand?

Thank you. I'm glad I came, too. No, she didn't go to jail. Her three-year sentence was suspended. Her probation terms included regular psychological counseling, work at a halfway house and no drinking. And her driver's license was suspended for five years.

Thank you. Take care of yourselves. All of you, please, please take care of yourselves.

What nice kids they are. I think if I'd told them about the fox, they'd have understood. They'd have appreciated how astonishing it was, when we'd never seen a fox before, to have one come and stand on the patio two days after Todd's death—just come and stand there staring at the kitchen window before it turned and slowly moved away.

Carole's pregnant sister came to be with her that afternoon. "I've been looking at a book of baby names," she said. "Did you know when you named Todd that it means 'fox'?"

Was Todd trying to tell us he's all right? I think these kids would understand how much we want to believe that.

Richard Morsilli with Jo Coudert

I Don't Want to Walk Without You

The only courage that matters is the kind that gets you from one moment to the next.

Mignon McLaughlin

From the time my daughter Jennifer was about three years old, we would sing to each other a line from an old Barry Manilow song about not wanting to walk without each other. Instead of the word "baby" I would sing "Jenny," and she would simultaneously say "Mommy." I was a single mom, and she was an only child. It became our pledge to each other . . . our lifeline of support through some difficult years.

Tragically, the day came when I had to walk without her. On a cold October evening in 1995, two Marine Corps officers made that fateful visit to my door to inform me that my nineteen-year-old daughter was dead.

Several weeks after the funeral, her belongings were shipped to me from her base. I stood alone weeping in my garage as the moving men unloaded thirty boxes of her things. Everything came back, except her.

It took several months before I could open some of the

boxes. I could only bear to go through one or two at a time. During one of these painful sortings, I found her black military dress shoes. Jennifer and I wore the same shoe size, so I put them on. Immediately, our old song popped into my head. I thought, *If I can wear Jen's shoes, particularly on days when I need to feel her close to me, this might be a way we could continue to "walk together."* Interestingly, they looked similar to the latest style for women's shoes, so it seemed like a possibility.

As excruciating as the holidays are without her, I find the two most difficult days are her birthday and the date of her death. Since her passing, I have chosen not to work on those two days. But in January 1998, I didn't have a choice.

I was scheduled to present a series of out-of-town broadcasts and seminars starting on Jennifer's birthday. As a public speaker and trainer, the emotional toll of this significant day was compounded by the demand from my audience to be constantly positive and motivational in my presentations. I wondered how I would ever get through the day. I decided to wear her military shoes that day. I wanted to feel her walking with me.

Somehow, the day came together. Everything seemed to go well. Even so, as I headed back to the hotel where I was staying, I felt very sad and lonely. A hotel was the last place I wanted to be that evening. I approached the front desk in the lobby to pick up a card that was waiting for me from my sister Jeanne. She knew how emotionally difficult Jen's birthday would be. As I was picking up my mail, I heard the bellman on the phone with a hotel guest. He was explaining that the hotel no longer had a shoe-shine person, but he would be glad to shine the shoes himself.

As a trainer in customer service, I was quite impressed with what I heard. When he got off the phone, I complimented him on his customer-service skills. He responded humbly,

"It's a quiet night. And besides, I was in the military. Shining shoes is one of my specialties." He looked down at mine and with a big smile said, "I'll be glad to do yours for you." I thanked him for the offer, but told him I didn't want to impose. He insisted, "If you change your mind, bring them down."

As I walked to my room, my thoughts flashed back to the time I first saw Jennifer in these shoes. It was at her graduation from boot camp at Parris Island. Jen had been selected the Honor Graduate for her platoon in recognition of outstanding "leadership, discipline, proficiency, bearing and physical fitness."

I can still see Jennifer as she was presented the medal. She stood at attention in her dress blues and these shoes. It was the proudest moment of my life. I knew the courage it took for her to accomplish all that she did, just as it took courage to do what I had to do today. I glanced down at the shoes. *I sure haven't kept these shoes looking as nice as Jen did,* I thought. They actually needed a good "spit shine." I thought how symbolic it would be to have them polished on her birthday, especially by someone who previously served in the military.

I changed into another pair of shoes and took Jen's down to the front desk. I told the bellman that I had decided to take him up on his offer. He smiled and said he would bring them up to my room when he was finished.

As I walked back, I wondered if I should share with him the significance of his gesture. These shoes played a key role in helping me get through the day. There's something symbolic about polishing and shining an item (whether it's a medal or a pair of shoes) as a way of acknowledging accomplishments, acts of courage and even birthdays. This young man helped me recognize all of this with his kindness.

When he knocked on the door a little while later, I

hesitated. There are times when words are just not adequate, and this was one of those moments. I opened the door, smiled and simply thanked him, telling him it meant a lot to me. I handed him a large tip.

I shut the door and stood cradling the shoes. Their polished surfaces shone back to me, just as Jen's face had that graduation day. I walked over to the table where I had placed a single rose in a bud vase next to Jennifer's picture. I put the shoes next to the rose and whispered, "Happy twenty-second birthday, Sweetheart. We found a way to continue to walk together after all."

Joyce A. Harvey

I Wish You Enough

Recently, I overheard a father and daughter in their last moments together. They had announced her departure and standing near the security gate, they hugged and he said, "I love you. I wish you enough."

She in turn said, "Daddy, our life together has been more than enough. Your love is all I ever needed. I wish you enough, too, Daddy." They kissed, and she left. He walked over toward the window where I was seated. Standing there I could see he wanted and needed to cry. I tried not to intrude on his privacy, but he welcomed me in by asking, "Did you ever say good-bye to someone knowing it would be forever?"

"Yes, I have," I replied. Saying that brought back memories I had of expressing my love and appreciation for all my dad had done for me. Recognizing that his days were limited, I took the time to tell him face-to-face how much he meant to me. So I knew what this man was experiencing. "Forgive me for asking, but why is this a forever good-bye?" I asked.

"I am old, and she lives much too far away. I have challenges ahead, and the reality is, the next trip back will be for my funeral," he said.

"When you were saying good-bye I heard you say, 'I wish you enough.' May I ask what that means?"

He began to smile. "That's a wish that has been handed down from other generations. My parents used to say it to everyone." He paused for a moment, and looking up as if trying to remember it in detail, he smiled even more. "When we said 'I wish you enough,' we were wanting the other person to have a life filled with just enough good things to sustain them," he continued and then turning toward me he recited the following:

I wish you enough sun to keep your attitude bright.
I wish you enough rain to appreciate the sun more.
I wish you enough happiness to keep your spirit alive.
I wish you enough pain so that the smallest joys in life appear much bigger.
I wish you enough gain to satisfy your wanting.
I wish you enough loss to appreciate all that you possess.
I wish you enough "hellos" to get you through the final "good-bye."

He then began to sob and walked away.
I wish you enough.

Bob Perks

The Quickening

"No, I haven't felt any movements yet," I responded with practiced pleasantness, which hid my anxiety and disappointment.

"Oh, well, I'm sure you'll feel those little feet and hands flutter inside any day now!"

Apparently, my attempts to conceal my own concerns about the health of my developing child were wearing thin. I was now six months along, gaining in weight and inches, yet feeling nothing going on inside. I could not dismiss the idea that something was not quite right. And according to the many texts I was reading, fetal movement could be detected by the mother as early as four months, so my fears grew.

I was haunted by the fact that this little baby had come to us as a surprise, and I had therefore not prepared his new home as a responsible and loving parent might have. I had inadvertently taken him to bars on weekends and to the Jacuzzi at night during his first few weeks. My husband, Jack, was taking strong medications to abate the relentless pain of a rare neurological disorder. So despite this adversity, a brave little soul decided to make his way into the world through us. Yet he would not move.

My husband and I were soon forced to think of other things as his mother's doctor told us the terrible news. She had just suffered a large intercranial hemorrhage that continued to bleed. This came as a heavy blow to all as she had been the arms, legs and voice of her husband, who had been crippled by a stroke nearly twenty years ago. It was almost unimaginable that my mother-in-law now lay in a hospital bed, writhing with the tremendous pain in her head as well as her heart, as she could not be home to care for her husband of fifty years.

Jack and I, along with his seven other siblings and their families, made daily visits to his mother's hospital room. These visitations were laden with sadness, making conversation even among the closest members strained. My own anxiety was again magnified by the many inquiries as to the progress of my pregnancy—which seemed the most appropriate subject to speak of when I was present among other family members. And with Jack's family being so large, the stories of how each grandchild came to be were recounted. In the case of each pregnancy and delivery of the eight grandchildren, there was building evidence that, indeed, my little child was having trouble. This thought was now paired with the possibility that my mother-in-law would never see this, her grandson, who would become the only bearer of the family name of the new generation.

And here before me lay the matriarch of so many families. A lady so kind and gentle that I felt immediate warmth and welcoming from her even upon our first introduction four years ago. I came to know how she was too lovely to ever say an unkind word to or about anyone. She spent her life raising a beautiful family and her later years quietly but tightly keeping everyone together.

And so, I thought, with much regret, that my little child may not know the softness of her cheek, the kindness of her eyes, the ever-present giggle in her words and the powerful love that radiates from this small yet extraordinary lady before me. Like silent, somber sentinels, each child in vigil by their mother's side, Patricia Ann Kiernan took her last breaths and passed away during the early morning hours. All then gathered at her home to comfort their father on that winter day.

Looking down to the events happening on Earth, a timid little boy holds tightly to the strong bars of a pearly gate. He releases the pressure of his grip for a moment as he strains his head to peer over the cloud's edge cautiously. He gazes down, curious about the people he sees, yet reluctant to leave his safe harbor. He quickly pulls himself back from the edge and examines the sparkling structure of the gate before him. Again and again he is drawn to watch the world below, yet steadfastly remains at his post.

Until he is approached by a beautiful lady. She walks slowly toward the boy, her arms open to embrace him, her face beaming with such joy at their meeting. She smiles so tenderly at him that the boy is immediately disarmed and raises his hand from the gate to meet her touch. Her arms envelop him, and he finds immediate comfort and security in her embrace.

"Little one," she says softly and kindly. "They are all waiting for you down there. Don't be frightened for you are already loved and will be taken very good care of. Hurry now, child! I promise you will have a wonderful time, and I will be waiting for you here when you return." She giggles and then gives him an extra-tight squeeze before opening her arms.

The little boy looks at her and smiles happily, trusting in all she has said. And now, growing more excited about the adventure that awaits him, he steps confidently onto the cloud's edge. He turns, waves to the beautiful lady—and jumps!

I sat on the last hallway stair, hearing the saddest, most lonely sobs of my father-in-law, who had just lost his best friend and the love of his life. The air inside this old house, with its thousand-and-one memories of happy times and years gone by, hung with pain and parting. My husband was at his father's side, his shiny blue eyes now tearful and dull.

My hands lay across my swollen belly in silence and sorrow. Until ... "tap, tap, tap."

My eyes grew wide. I listened quietly with my entire body.

"Tick. Tick. Tap. Tap."

Like Morse code came movement inside! I sat smiling and enjoying this moment to myself. "There you are! There you are!" I exclaimed to the tapping. I was so relieved and excited. I was thrilled that this moment had finally come! And yet the gravity of the day prevented me from shouting out to everyone, "He's here! He's here!" Instead, I thanked God in a whispered prayer and found my husband on the porch.

"He just kicked," I said quietly to Jack. Jack looked back at me for a moment, and then his eyes lit up as he announced to everyone excitedly, "The baby just kicked for the first time!" I smiled and giggled as his sisters turned toward me and, forgetting their loss for a moment, joined in our happiness.

And as the day wore on, my previous worries now vanishing, I reflected on the happenings of the morning. Of how with the passing of one life, another is ushered in. And I thought again of how, perhaps, instead of no longer being alive in time to see our very happy and healthy baby boy, his grandmother was really the *first* to see him. And this will be how I begin to tell my son what a wonderful grandmother he has!

Monica Kiernan

The Horizon

Life is eternal, and love is immortal,
and death is only a horizon;
and a horizon is nothing save the limit of our sight.

Rossiter Worthington Raymond

I am standing upon the seashore.
A ship at my side spreads her white sails to the morning
breeze and starts for the blue ocean.
She is an object of beauty and strength.
I stand and watch her until at length she hangs like a
speck of white cloud on the horizon,
Just where the sea and the sky come to mingle with one
another.
Then someone at my side says: "There, she is gone."
"Gone where?"
Gone from my sight. That is all.
She is just as large in mast and hull and spar as she was
when she left my side,
And she is just as able to bear her load of living freight to
her destined port.
Her diminished size is in me, not in her.

And just at the moment when someone at my side says,
"There, she is gone," there are other eyes watching her
   coming,
And other voices ready to take up the glad shout:
"Here she comes!"
And that is dying.

Henry Scott Holland

6

INSIGHTS AND LESSONS

You're Still Here

At the finest level of my being,
you're still with me.
We still look at each other,
at that level beyond sight.
We talk and laugh with each other,
in a place beyond words.
We still touch each other,
on a level beyond touch.
We share time together in a place,
where time stands still.
We are still together,
on a level called Love.
But I cry alone for you,
in a place called reality.

Richard Lepinsky

Chocolate-Covered Cherries

The experience of grief is a great gift . . . for the heart that breaks is just opening again.

Sharon Callahan

What a terrible way to spend Christmas. My oldest son, Cameron, had been diagnosed with acute myeloblastic leukemia the previous June. After a harrowing ride in a military helicopter to Walter Reed Hospital, three rounds of horrendous chemotherapy, an excruciating lung re-section and a disappointing bone-marrow search, we were at Duke University Hospital. Cameron had undergone a cord-blood transplant, a last-ditch effort to save his life, in early December. Now, here it was Christmas Eve.

Spending Christmas in the small room on Ward 9200 seemed strange—so different from our usual holiday set-ting at home. We had always spent weeks on our favorite holiday project: baking cookies. Now the cookies were sent from family and friends since I tried to spend all my time with Cameron, helping to ease the long, tedious hours. He had been in isolation for weeks because the chemotherapy and drugs left him with no immune system. When presents arrived in the mail, we didn't wait for Christmas, but opened them immediately—anything to create a bright moment in that dull and painful time.

Always in the past, 6:00 P.M. on Christmas Eve was the "Magic Hour." This was the time when everyone in my family in Iowa, Wisconsin, California and Washington, D.C., opened our presents. We all did this at exactly the same time, somehow bringing the family together, even though we lived so far apart. Cameron's father, stepmother, sister and brother also opened presents at their house at that time.

This year, the Magic Hour would find just Cameron and me in a small, almost-bare hospital room, since most decorations weren't allowed in the sterile environment.

We sat together, listening to the drone of the HEPA filter and the beeping of the six infusion pumps hooked to a catheter in his heart, as Cameron waited until 6:00 P.M. exactly to open the few presents I had saved aside for him. He insisted we follow this small tradition to create some semblance of normalcy—all of which had been abruptly abandoned six months earlier. I watched him open the presents. His favorite was a Hug Me Elmo toy that said "I love you" when he squeezed it.

All too quickly, Christmas was over. Or so I thought.

Cameron carefully reached over the side of his hospital bed and handed me a small green box. It was wrapped beautifully, obviously by a gift store, with perfect edges and a folded piece of ribbon held with a gold embossed sticker.

Surprised, I said, "For me?"

"Mom, it wouldn't be Christmas unless you have something to unwrap, too."

I was speechless. Finally, I asked, "But how did you get this? Did you ask a nurse to run down to the gift store?"

Cameron leaned back in his bed and gave me his most

devilish smile. "Nope. Yesterday, when you went home for a few hours to take a shower, I sneaked downstairs."

"CAMERON! You aren't supposed to leave the floor! You know you're susceptible to almost any germ. They let you leave the ward?"

"Nope!" His smile was even bigger now. "They weren't looking. I just walked out."

This was no small feat since he could barely walk, and certainly not unassisted. It took every ounce of strength just to cruise the small ward halls, pushing the heavy IV pole hung with medication and a pain pump. How could he possibly have made it nine floors to the gift store?

"Don't worry, Mom. I wore my mask, and I used the cane. Man, they really chewed me out when I got back. I couldn't sneak back in, since they'd been looking for me."

I couldn't look up. I held the box even tighter now and had already started to cry.

"Open it. It's not much, but it wouldn't be Christmas if you didn't have something from me to unwrap."

I opened the box of gift-store-wrapped chocolate-covered cherries. "They are your favorite, right?" he asked hopefully.

I finally looked at my poor eighteen-year-old baby. Cameron had begun all this suffering almost immediately after his high-school graduation. Did he know how much he was teaching me about what being a family really meant? "Oh, absolutely my favorite!"

Cameron chuckled a little bit. "See, we still have our traditions—even in here."

"Cameron, this is the best present I've ever received—ever," I told him, and I meant every word. "Let's start a new tradition. Every Christmas, let's only give each other a box of chocolate-covered cherries, and we'll reminisce about the year we spent Christmas at Duke University Hospital battling leukemia. We'll remember how horrible it all was, and how glad we are that it is finally over."

We made that pact right then and there, as we shared the box of chocolate-covered cherries. What a wonderful way to spend Christmas!

Cameron died two months later, after two unsuccessful cord-blood transplants. He was so brave—never giving in, never giving up. On my first Christmas without him I sent a special present to friends and family with this note:

"This is my gift to you—a box of chocolate-covered cherries. And when you open it, I hope it will remind you what the holidays are really about—being with your friends and family—recreating traditions, maybe starting some new ones—but most of all—love."

What a beautiful way to spend Christmas.

Dawn Holt

Remember with Courage

Christmas is a special time of year. And while pretty packages and twinkling lights are the window dressing for this exciting festivity, it is the warmth and love of family that make the holiday season so memorable. However, it can be a painful time for those experiencing the recent loss of a loved one.

Twelve years ago, my husband died suddenly. Although it was only the end of October, department stores glittered with decorations and staff worked eagerly to jump-start sales. When purchasing outfits for my ten- and twelve-year-old daughters to wear to their father's funeral, the salesclerk innocently asked if I was getting an early start on my Christmas shopping. I shall never forget the piercing pain in my heart as I stumbled for an answer.

I drove home in tears, realizing just how out of sync I was with the outside world. The holiday momentum was building, and I felt as though I was being swallowed by a huge black hole. I wanted to scream. I wanted the world to stop spinning. I wanted to run away . . . find some place that wasn't dripping with tinsel and holiday cheer. But more than anything, I wanted my family back.

The following weeks passed, and December twenty-fifth

approached quickly. I struggled with wanting to dismiss Christmas and yet, at the same time, to embrace the childhood excitement my daughters were beginning to brim with. While it was easy for me to sustain resentment toward the outside world, it was impossible to resist them. They made their annual wish list and insisted on decorating the house. Through their actions, it became abundantly clear that Christmas was going to happen whether I wanted it to or not.

My girls taught me more about grieving than I could have ever taught them. They missed their dad terribly. Yet they were able to perceive the enchantment of Christmas as they had in years prior, albeit in a different way. It was obvious they'd made a choice to participate in the ardor of Christmas. Being children, they may not have been aware of the implications of this choice. Perhaps that was the saving grace. By making an unconscious choice they were relieved of any damning self-judgment that would cite disrespect to their father's memory. They instinctively knew their lives had to go on, and they showed me that mine had to as well.

Christmas did go on for us that year. And yes, it was very different. The three of us pulled together as a family and developed new traditions to help face the day. For instance, we hung a picture of my husband in the Christmas tree, declaring him our "Christmas Star." We also dedicated Christmas Eve as the day to honor him by making a visit to the cemetery. It was there that I presented each daughter with one of our wedding bands as a gift from both their father and me. We returned home for a quiet evening to reminisce about our favorite family times together. The tears flowed, at times uncontrollably, but in a very healing way.

Surprisingly, Christmas Day was quite pleasant. It was not filled with the heavy sadness or feelings of sorrow that

I'd anticipated. Instead, it was filled with love and compassion. We invited our extended family and close friends to spend the day with us. During dinner, we exchanged stories of years gone by, many of them bringing smiles and laughter to everyone.

In reflection, I am thankful we found the courage to embrace Christmas that year. In doing so, we renewed our strength and courage to go on and live our lives as we were meant to. Two years later, my daughters and I were blessed to receive a new family, complete with a dad and three more children.

Today, we embrace Christmas as a way of celebrating not only those we are fortunate to have in our lives, but to also remember those we hold so dearly in our hearts.

If you are facing Christmas alone for the first time, I encourage you to reach out to someone you trust and share your feelings with them. Devote a time and place prior to Christmas Day in which you can openly honor your loved one and acknowledge your feelings. Finally, on Christmas Day, intentionally set your focus on family and friends who not only share in your loss, but who bring precious gifts of love and support to aid you in your healing journey.

You are not alone, although you may feel this way. Many people have been where you are, and we care deeply.

Janelle M. Breese Biagioni

My Father's Voice

My father raised me mostly by example. He was a doctor who also had a farm in the Midwest on which he raised cattle, horses and hunting dogs. I learned by watching how to work; how to handle animals and the kinds of unforeseen events that are so frequent in the life of a doctor's family.

My father took things as they came, dealt with them and, as he used to say when some obstacle had been overcome, "Let's move right along." He had a few precepts I was expected to live by, and he always referred to them by their combined initial letters: DL! DC! SDT! and DPB! They stood for Don't Lie; Don't Cheat; Slow Down and Think; and Don't Panic, Bud! I was amazed as a boy how often he found occasion to say one or another of those things.

He thought animals were splendid teachers, and he taught me to watch them carefully. One winter a squirrel invaded our house around Thanksgiving. We never saw or heard it, but I found stashes of nuts hidden under the cushions of the couch and almost every chair. The fascinating thing is that the nuts were always one of a kind. Acorns in my father's chair. Hickory nuts at one end of the sofa and almonds in their shells—stolen from the holiday bowl that my mother kept on the coffee table.

I thought the squirrel was very smart to sort out his larder that way. My dad said the squirrel was even smarter than I had imagined and gathered only one kind of nut at a time. And that would be much more efficient than gathering a mix and then having to sort them out.

That kind of teaching did not alter much even when I was a grown man, even to the day he died. I was thirty when he became ill on Christmas Eve. We buried him on the third of January, his coffin draped in an American flag. The United States soldier who received the folded flag from the bearers handed it to me without a word. I clutched it to my heart as my wife and I left that most sorrowful of places for the long, forlorn drive to the airport.

The world seemed darkened by his absence. There was an emptiness so great that at times I thought I could not bear it. At his funeral, the minister told me that all he had been to me still lived. He said if I listened I could hear what my father's response would be to any concern I needed to bring him. But after I left the small country town where he lived and returned to the large city where I was making my way, I never once heard his voice. Never once. That troubled me deeply. When I was worried about leaving one job for another—something I would have talked over with my dad—I tried to imagine that we were sitting in his barn having one of our "life-talks," as my mother used to call them. But there was only silence and the image of me alone, waiting and profoundly sad.

Although I worked in the city, my wife and I bought an old farmhouse on a few acres of land some forty miles away. It had a pond where I could teach my son to fish and a meadow where we could work our dog.

One day during the same dreadful winter that I lost my father, I set out with my young son to do a few errands. We drove out into the country to look at some antique dining-room chairs I was thinking of buying as a surprise for my wife. I said we'd be home by suppertime. We had gone a few miles when my son saw deer grazing just beyond the edge of a parking lot that belonged to our country church. I pulled in the lot, turned off the engine and let the car glide as close to the deer as I could without spooking them.

A buck and three does rummaged in the snow for grass and leaves. They occasionally raised their heads and took a long slow read of the air. They knew, of course, we were there. They just wanted to be certain they were safe.

We were as still as we could be and watched them for some time. When I took my son's hand and turned around to leave, I saw a pall of smoke coming from under the hood of my car. We stopped in our tracks. *Oh God,* I thought, *the engine is on fire. And I am alone with a child in the middle of winter in the middle of nowhere.* I did not have a cell phone.

I told my son to stay where he was, and I went to the car to investigate. I opened the driver's door, pulled the hood latch and went to the front of the car. Gingerly, I opened the hood. As soon as I did, I saw that the right front of the engine was aglow with fire, and smoke was coming out of it at a pretty good clip. I closed the hood without latching it down and went to where my son stood in the snow, excited and amazed.

"Daddy, is the car gonna blow up?"

"No. But I sure have to do something, and I don't know what. . . ."

"Snow will put it out," he said.

"Snow might crack a cylinder, too." *What could be the matter?* I thought. *Engines just don't catch fire like that.* My mind began to move irrationally. I would have to find a house along the road, call for help. I would have to call my wife, frighten her probably. There would be the expense of the tow and probably a new engine. Then as clearly as I ever heard it in my life, I heard my dad say, "DPB!"

I am still astonished that I was immediately calmed. The frantic racing of my mind ceased. I decided to see exactly what, in fact, was burning. I retrieved a stick from a little oak and went to the car, opened the hood and poked at the glowing red place on the engine. Coals fell from it, through to the ground. I could see then, sitting on the engine block in a perfect little circle—a small collection of acorns, cradled by the shape of the metal.

I laughed out loud. "Come here," I said to my son. "Look, a squirrel stowed its treasure in our car. And when the engine got hot, his acorns got roasted."

I knocked the acorns and the rest of the glowing coals off the engine, closed the hood, put my son in his car seat and got in beside him.

When we drove away to finish our errand, I knew—for the first time since my dad died—that I could get on with my life. For on that snowy day in the parking lot of our country church, I discovered that his voice was still in my heart, and his lessons would be with me forever.

Walker Meade

Missing Pa

Honest listening is one of the best medicines we can offer the dying and the bereaved.

Jean Cameron

One day my four-year-old son Sam told me he'd seen his babysitter crying because she'd broken up with her boyfriend. "She was sad," he explained. "I've never been sad," Sam added. "Not ever."

It was true. Sam's life was happy in large part because of his relationship with my father. As Sam told everyone, Pa Hood was more than a grandfather to him—they were buddies.

There's a scene in the movie *Anne of Green Gables* in which Anne wishes aloud for a bosom friend. Watching that one day, Sam sat up and declared, "That's me and Pa—bosom friends forever and ever."

My father described their relationship the same way. When I went out of town one night a week to teach, it was Pa in his red pickup truck who'd meet Sam at school and take him back to his house. There they'd play pirates and knights and Robin Hood.

They even dressed alike: pocket T-shirts, baseball caps and jeans. They had special restaurants they frequented, playgrounds where they were regulars, and toy stores where Pa allowed Sam to race up and down the aisles on motorized cars.

Sam had even memorized my father's phone number and called him every morning and night. "Pa," he would ask, clutching the phone, "can I call you ten hundred more times?" Pa always said yes and answered the phone every time with equal delight.

Then my father became ill. In the months he was hospitalized for lung cancer, I worried about how Sam would react to Pa's condition: the needle bruises, the oxygen tubes, his weakened state. When I explained to Sam that seeing Pa so sick might scare him, he was surprised. "He could never scare me," Sam said.

Later I watched adults approach my father's hospital bed with trepidation, unsure of what to say or do. But Sam knew exactly what was right: hugs and jokes, as always.

"Are you coming home soon?" he'd ask.

"I'm trying," Pa would tell him.

When my dad died, everything changed for me and Sam. Not wanting to confront the questions and feelings my father's death raised, I kept my overwhelming sadness at bay. When well-meaning people asked how I was doing, I'd give them a short answer and swiftly change the subject.

Sam was different, however. For him, wondering aloud was the best way to understand.

"So," he'd say, settling in his car seat, "Pa's in space, right?" Or, pointing at a stained-glass window in church, he'd ask, "Is one of those angels Pa?"

"Where's heaven?" Sam asked right after my father died.

"No one knows exactly," I said. "Lots of people think it's in the sky."

"No," Sam said, shaking his head, "it's very far away. Near Cambodia."

"When you die," he asked on another afternoon, "you disappear, right? And when you faint, you only disappear a little. Right?"

I thought his questions were good. The part I had trouble with was what he always did afterward: He'd look me right in the eye with more hope than I could stand and wait for my approval or correction or wisdom. But in this matter my fear and ignorance were so large that I'd grow dumb in the face of his innocence.

Remembering Sam's approach to my father's illness, I began to watch his approach to grief. At night he'd press his face against his bedroom window and cry, calling out into the darkness, "Pa, I love you! Sweet dreams!" Then, after his tears stopped, he'd climb into bed, somehow satisfied, and sleep. I, however, would wander the house all night, not knowing how to mourn.

One day in the supermarket parking lot, I saw a red truck like my father's. For an instant I forgot he had died. My heart leapt as I thought, *Dad's here!*

Then I remembered and succumbed to an onslaught of tears. Sam climbed onto my lap and jammed himself between me and the steering wheel.

"You miss Pa, don't you?" he asked.

I managed to nod.

"You have to believe he's with us, Mommy," he said. "You have to believe that."

Too young to attach to a particular ideology, Sam was simply dealing with grief and loss by believing that death does not really separate us from those we love. I couldn't show him heaven on a map or explain the course a soul might travel. But he'd found his own way to cope.

Recently while I was cooking dinner, Sam sat by himself at the kitchen table, quietly coloring in his Spider Man coloring book. "I love you, too," he said.

I laughed and said, "You only say 'I love you, too' after someone says 'I love you' first."

"I know," Sam said. "Pa just said, 'I love you, Sam,' and I said, 'I love you, too.'" He kept coloring.

"Pa just talked to you?" I asked.

"Oh, Mommy," Sam said, "he tells me he loves me every day. He tells you, too. You're just not listening."

Again, I have begun to take Sam's lead. I have begun to listen.

Ann Hood
Originally published in Parenting *magazine*

THE FAMILY CIRCUS® By Bil Keane

"... and say hi to our grandfather
who art in heaven, too."

What Death Has Taught Me

My phone rang at 7:20 A.M., July 23, 2000. As I picked it up, a feeling of foreboding came over me, as usually happens when the phone rings at an odd hour. It was my father . . . there's been an accident . . . it's Joe . . . it's bad . . . he's been killed. Joe is my nephew, the son of my sister. He was killed in a car accident . . . and so the journey begins.

Joe turned eighteen on February 20, 2000. He was looking forward to heading off to university the following year, the first in our family to do so. He was going to take kinesiology, and he was going to be amazing.

For one year, I searched for answers, as many do when they lose someone they love. For one year, I was sad with a pit of emptiness in my stomach. Oh, sometimes on the outside I would appear to be okay, but inside the pit was always there.

Then one day in May 2001 . . . I realized I was on a journey. What I realized is below:

When you lose someone you love, your soul moves to another "place." This "place" is shared only by others who have also lost someone they love. You know they're "there" by the look in their eyes when they tell you how sorry they are for your loss. They have traveled the "journey" you are about to travel and know the emptiness you feel. This "place" is where your life seems to stand still for a while. You are still physically here, yet you sense you're just not "here" right now.

To the observer, your life is carrying on. Inside, however, those who have been "there" know you're still on a journey for a time. You think it must be time for you to "come back" now, and for short periods you do. Then some thing, some place, some song sends you on "journey" again.

Those who have been "there" can journey with you for a time if you let them. Company on a journey is sometimes helpful, and sometimes you must journey alone.

The road on your journey has been much traveled. There are hills to climb, corners to go around and potholes to get through. Flat tires to repair, and tanks gone empty that need refilling. Most welcomed on the journey are the straight stretches. They allow you to coast easily and build up again to approach the next hill with a bit more ease.

As time goes on, the hills become smaller, and the road on your journey does lead you "home" again. At first for short periods of time, and eventually for much longer times. It is a different "home" now and a different "you" now. You will have traveled far and experienced much, and your eyes . . . your eyes will speak of your journey. You'll be ready then to guide another, look in their eyes and say, "I am *so* sorry for your loss."

"Death" has taught me many things. Things that, if listed, would fill pages time wouldn't permit to be read. For today, it's taught me:

To hold onto my children a little longer and a little tighter when we hug.

To hold onto my friends a little longer and a little tighter when we hug.

That I'm not being silly telling my children I love them every day.

To hug my children even when they don't seem to want to be hugged (like in public!).

To treasure bedtime chats, stories of friends and sharing inner thoughts.

That fingerprints on the wall are dirt to one and treasures to another.

That I'll not wait to do things, and I'll not wait to say things.

To be happy today in the journey.

That life is short and meant to be experienced and celebrated every day that we're here.

That we have a choice in the death of those we love, to honor their death with anger or to honor it with our life and living it to the fullest.

Most importantly, death has taught me to live.

Barb Kerr

Keep Your Fork

For what is it to die, but to stand in the sun and melt into the wind? And when the Earth has claimed our limbs, then we shall truly dance.

Kahlil Gibran

The sound of Martha's voice on the other end of the telephone always brought a smile to Brother Jim's face. She was not only one of the oldest members of the congregation, but one of the most faithful. Aunt Martie, as all the children called her, just seemed to ooze faith, hope and love wherever she went.

This time, however, there seemed to be an unusual tone to her words.

"Preacher, could you stop by this afternoon? I need to talk with you."

"Of course. I'll be there around three. Is that okay?"

As they sat facing each other in the quiet of her small living room, Jim learned the reason for what he sensed in her voice. Martha told him that her doctor had just discovered a previously undetected tumor.

"He says I probably have six months to live." Martha's

words were certainly serious, yet there was a definite calm about her.

"I'm so sorry to . . ." but before Jim could finish, Martha interrupted.

"Don't be. The Lord has been good. I have lived a long life. I'm ready to go. You know that."

"I know," Jim whispered with a reassuring nod.

"But I do want to talk with you about my funeral. I have been thinking about it, and there are things that I want."

The two talked quietly for a long time. They talked about Martha's favorite hymns, the passages of Scripture that had meant so much to her through the years, and the many memories they shared from the five years Jim had been with Central Church.

When it seemed that they had covered just about everything, Aunt Martie paused, looked up at Jim with a twinkle in her eye, and then added, "One more thing, Preacher. When they bury me, I want my old Bible in one hand and a fork in the other."

"A fork?" Jim was sure he had heard everything, but this caught him by surprise. "Why do you want to be buried with a fork?"

"I have been thinking about all of the church dinners and banquets that I attended through the years," she explained. "I couldn't begin to count them all. But one thing sticks in my mind.

"At those really nice get-togethers, when the meal was almost finished, a server or maybe the hostess would come by to collect the dirty dishes. I can hear the words now. Sometimes, at the best ones, somebody would lean over my shoulder and whisper, 'You can keep your fork.'

"And do you know what that meant? Dessert was coming!

"It didn't mean a cup of Jell-O or pudding or even a dish of ice cream. You don't need a fork for that. It meant the good stuff, like chocolate cake or cherry pie! When they told me I could keep my fork, I knew the best was yet to come!

"That's exactly what I want people to talk about at my funeral. Oh, they can talk about all the good times we had together. That would be nice.

"But when they walk by my casket and look at my pretty blue dress, I want them to turn to one another and say, 'Why the fork?'

"That's what I want to say. I want you to tell them that I kept my fork because the best is yet to come."

Dr. Roger William Thomas

7

LIVING AGAIN

I can choose to sit in perpetual sadness, immobilized by the gravity of my loss, or I can choose to rise from the pain and treasure the most precious gift I have—life itself.

Walter Anderson

Lilyfish

After the world takes an eggbeater to your soul, you never know what's going to get you up and back among the living. In my case, it was the ham. It was 3:30 on a sweltering July afternoon, three weeks to the hour since my new baby daughter lay down for a nap and woke up on the other side of this life.

I decided it was time to go fishing. There were any number of good reasons. For one, I could sit still and smell Lily's baby sweetness in the corners of the house, still feel her small heft in the hollow of my shoulder. For another, I'd hardly left the house since she died and had taken to working my way through an alarming amount of dark rum and tonic each night, not a sustainable grief-management technique over the long haul. Jane and I had planted the memorial pink crepe myrtle and the yellow lilies, chosen for having the audacity to bloom in the heat of the summer, the very time Lily died.

But it was the ham that got me off the dime. After the funeral, the neighbors had started bringing over hog's hind legs as if the baby might rise from the dead and stop by for a sandwich if they could just get enough cured pork in the refrigerator. I knew my mind wasn't quite right, knew I still hadn't even accepted her death. But it seemed like I'd lose it unless I put some distance between me and the ham.

I shoved a small box of lures in a fanny pack, spooled up a spinning rod with six-pound mono line and filled a quart bottle with tap water. On my way out the door, I stopped, as I have taken to doing since her death, to touch the tiny blue urn on the mantel. "Baby girl," I said. I stood there for several minutes, feeling the coolness of fired clay and waiting for my eyes to clear again. Then I got in the car and drove twenty miles north of Washington, D.C., to the Seneca Breaks on the upper Potomac River.

I didn't particularly care that it was 102 degrees outside. I didn't particularly care that any smallmouth bass not yet parboiled by the worst heat wave in memory would scarcely be biting. I was furious at the world and everything still living in it now that my daughter wasn't alive. As I drove, the radio reported severe thunderstorms to the west and said they might be moving our way. Fine by me. If someone up there wanted to send a little electroshock therapy my way, I'd be easy to find.

Even at five o'clock the sun still had its noon fury. The heat had emptied the normally crowded parking lot at the river's edge. I stepped out of the air-conditioned car into the afternoon's slow oven. I slugged down some water, put my long-billed cap on, found a wading stick in the underbrush and walked into the river. The water was bathtub warm and two feet below normal. Seneca Breaks, normally a mile-long series of fishy-looking riffles and rock gardens, was like the only angler fool enough to be out there—a ghost of its former self. At least it didn't smell like ham. But the fish weren't here, and I realized I shouldn't be either. It dawned on me that I'd better get in the water that went over my waist or risk heatstroke.

Just upstream from the breaks, the river is called Seneca Lake, three miles of deep flats covered with mats of floating grass. I worked my way out to the head of the breaks and slipped into this deeper water, casting a four-inch plastic worm on a light sinker. Soon I'd waded out chin-deep into the lake, holding my rod arm just high enough to keep the reel out of the water. There were bait fish dimpling the surface every so often and dragonflies landing on my wrist, and once a small brown water snake wriggled by so close I could have touched him.

Nothing was hitting my worm, but that was to be expected. My arms seemed to be working the rod on their own, and I was content to let them. I stood heron-still and felt the slow current brush grass against my legs. Every so often, a minnow would pucker up and take a little nip at my exposed leg. It tickled. Baby fish. I remembered how I'd call her Lilyfish sometimes when changing her diaper, remembered how she loved to be naked and squiggling on the changing table, gazing up at me and gurgling with something approaching rapture as I pulled at her arms and legs to stretch them.

The tears welled up again. I found the melody to an old Pete Townsend song running circles through my head about how the fire was gone, but it still burned. It would always burn. And that's how it was all right. The memories—her smell, her smile, the weight of her in my arms—would always smolder. And I'd always yearn for the one thing I'd never have.

And what struck me as I stood alone in the middle of the river was that while my world had been changed forever, the world itself had not changed a whit. The river simply went about its business. A dead catfish, bloated and colorless, washed serenely past on its way back down the food chain. The sun hammered down, and a hot wind wandered the water.

I caught a bluegill, then two little smallmouth bass, within ten minutes of each other. As I brought the fish to the surface, I had the sensation of bringing creatures from a parallel universe into my own for a minute before sending them darting back home. I wondered if death might be like this, traveling to a place where you didn't think it was possible to breathe, only to arrive discovering that you could. I hoped it was. The older I get, the more I believe there is such a thing as a soul, that energy changes form but still retains something it never loses. I hoped that Lily's soul was safe. That she knew how much she was still loved.

I don't know how long I stayed there or even if I kept fishing. I remember looking up at some point and noticing that the light had softened. It was after eight, and the sun was finally headed into the trees. And now, just like every summer night for eons, the birds came out: an osprey flying recon fifty feet over the shallows; a great blue heron flapping deep and slow, straight toward me out of the fireball, settling atop a rock and locking into hunting stance. And everywhere swallows were coming out like twinkling spirits to test who could trace the most intricate patterns in the air, trailing their liquid songs behind them.

Suddenly, I wasn't angry anymore. This is the world, I realized for the millionth time, and its unfathomable mystery, always and never the same, composed in roughly equal parts of suffering and wonder, unmoved by either, endlessly rolling away. It was getting dark now, hard to see the stones beneath the water. I waded carefully back to my car, rested the stick by a post for another fisherman to use, changed into dry clothes and drove home.

Take your grief one day at a time, someone had told me. I hadn't known what he meant at the time, but I did now. This had been a good day. Lily, you are always in my heart.

Bill Heavey

Hope Is Stronger Than Sorrow

Light always follows darkness.

Anonymous

In a quiet room away from the noise of the emergency room, I gazed at my four-month-old son Heath. As tears streamed down my face, I kissed his soft cheeks and stroked his downy blond hair. "How am I going to live without you?" I sobbed.

Just that morning, he had been laughing, but now my heart shattered as I envisioned everything he would never experience, everything I'd miss. I'd never see him take his first steps or hear him say, "I love you, Mommy!" There'd be no first day of school or wedding to look forward to. Looking into the future, all I saw was sorrow. I didn't think I could go on. But in time, I would learn that hope is stronger than sorrow. . . .

Before Bob and I were married eleven years ago, I learned after a routine exam that my kidneys weren't functioning.

"You have chronic renal failure," my doctor told me.

Stunned, I asked, "Am I going to die?"

He assured me that with a change in diet, I could live a normal life. Relieved, Bob and I made plans for our future. We wanted a baby right away, but first we saved to buy a house. One year later, we bought a lovely home in a lovely neighborhood. The time was right to have a baby, we happily decided.

But my doctor cautioned me, "If you become pregnant, the strain could worsen your condition to the point where you'll need dialysis or a transplant."

Later, I sobbed to Bob, "We'll never have a family now!"

"Then we'll adopt," he soothed.

Hope filled me, and I focused on staying healthy. But gradually, just walking up a flight of stairs exhausted me, and at night, twelve hours of sleep wasn't enough.

"Your kidneys have gotten weaker," my doctor explained. "You need a kidney transplant."

My name was put on a donor list, and I prayed that a kidney would be found soon. Thirteen months later, the hospital called.

"We have a donor," the transplant coordinator said. A man had died in a car accident, and I prayed that his family would find comfort in knowing their loved one had given the gift of life.

The surgery was a success, and I felt more alive than ever. *Your gift has given me a second chance,* I wrote in a letter of thanks to the donor family. *I'll always be grateful.*

As my body healed, my dream of having a baby was rekindled. I was elated when my doctor told me that it was safe for me to get pregnant now. He assured me the antirejection drugs I took wouldn't harm a baby I was carrying. But there were risks: Pregnancy could put a strain on my new kidney, I could have a rejection episode, or my baby could be born prematurely.

"We have to have faith that everything will be all right,"

Bob said.

And he was—I became pregnant a year and a half later. It was a healthy pregnancy until my seventh month, when I was at the hospital for a routine kidney test—and my water broke.

It's too soon! I anguished. *Please don't let me lose my baby!* Two hours later, Heath was born. Though tiny, he was healthy. As I held him in my arms I wept, "You're my miracle baby."

Every day with Heath was a reason to rejoice. From the way he held my finger while he drank his bottle to his sweet gurgles when I picked him up, he filled my heart with love. I couldn't have been happier. But then tragedy struck.

Just a few hours after I'd kissed my baby good-bye and gone to work, the police called to tell me that Heath, who had been with a sitter, had stopped breathing.

Numb with fear, I rushed to the hospital, praying that he'd be okay. He wasn't.

"I'm sorry," the doctor said. "Heath died of SIDS."

Bob and I were numb with grief and shock as we said good-bye to our son.

How can I go on? I agonized.

Before we left the hospital, a social worker talked with us about donating Heath's organs. In a strange twist of fate, I suddenly understood in a way I couldn't have before how my donor's family must have felt when faced with the decision Bob and I were being asked to make now. *Can I be as selfless?* I wondered.

But in the depths of my grief, I realized that in giving someone else new life, a part of my son would live on.

"I want to donate Heath's organs," I told Bob. He agreed. Later, doctors decided that Heath's corneas were the best option for donation.

Someone will see because of my son! I realized. It brought me some comfort, but I still grieved for the baby we had loved and lost. Just looking at Heath's picture tore at my heart.

I tried to go on by throwing myself into work. But every night I prayed, please don't let me wake up in the morning. When I did awake, I cried and cried.

Bob was hurting, too, so we joined a bereavement group. At the first meeting, I cried quietly while other parents talked about their grief. When it was my turn, I wept, "I miss being a mother."

One woman said, "I know what you're going through." Knowing they understood helped ease our pain, and seeing how some members had healed gave me hope. And in time, Bob and I knew we needed to go on with our lives. When we'd donated Heath's corneas, we'd decided to give someone a second chance. Now we needed to give ourselves the gift of life—and hope—again. So we decided to have another child.

When I became pregnant again, I was elated, but also very frightened. What if we lose this baby, too? I worried. And when I went into labor seven weeks early, my mind reeled.

"Just like Heath!" I sobbed.

Though she weighed just two and a half pounds, Savannah was perfect. But I worried, *What if she dies from SIDS, too?*

As a precaution, Savannah came home with a monitor that would alert us if she stopped breathing. But I constantly checked on her anyway. As the months passed and Savannah thrived, I began to relax.

Still, I knew I wouldn't find peace of mind until Savannah was out of danger. That happy day came when she was almost one, and she no longer needed the monitor. Her first birthday party was a celebration of life and a return of happiness.

Today, Savannah is three, and she fills our home with joy. And when I look at pictures of Heath, I smile instead of sob.

Someday, I'll tell Savannah about the donor program and how my life has been blessed because of it. But for now, I'm just looking forward to watching my daughter grow. And because of the gift of life I received, I won't miss one special moment.

Duane Shearer
As told to Janice Finnell
Previously appeared in Woman's World

The Miracle of Gary's Gift

Before he left for work, my husband, Gary, always told me, "Love you." But that day, he left before I was awake.

Looking back I wish I had gotten up to kiss him good-bye. But how could I know I'd never get another chance?

For a long time, memories like these tore at my heart. Then five very special people helped me heal.

Gary and I had met sixteen years earlier on a blind date. We fell in love, and five months later, we were married. After our sons, Jerrod and Casey, came along, our happiness was complete. I taught school, and Gary worked as a welder. I loved our life together.

Then just before noon that morning, the phone rang.

"Gary fell from a beam at the construction site," one of his coworkers said. "He's in ER."

Don't let him be badly hurt! I prayed. But at the hospital, a doctor told me that Gary had a severe head injury and needed surgery.

After the surgery, I was allowed to see Gary. "I'm here!" I choked.

He squeezed my hand, and I filled with hope. But by morning, his condition worsened and doctors induced a coma to reduce the swelling in his brain.

I brought the boys to see him. "Daddy's on a machine to help him breathe, so he can't talk," I said. "But you can talk to him."

Hearing the boys plead, "Please get well!" I couldn't contain my tears.

Six days after the accident, the doctor told me, "I'm sorry . . . Gary is brain-dead."

As grief tore through me, the doctor asked if I'd considered organ donation. Gary and I had never discussed it, but I thought about the kind of man he'd been. Always ready to help, he'd volunteered at church and chopped firewood for neighbors during a snowstorm. I knew what he would want.

Taking Gary's hand, I wept, "I'll raise the boys in a way that will make you proud. I'll miss you."

That day, Gary gave five people the gift of life.

After the funeral, despair engulfed me. But my sons needed me, so I forced myself to get up in the morning. I went through the motions at work. At home, I hid my tears every time I set the table for three instead of four.

The boys were suffering, too. Jerrod, fifteen, grew quiet, and Casey, eleven, lost his quick smile.

The only tiny solace was the hope that Gary had helped others. But I didn't know who the recipients were, and I was afraid to find out.

Then, a few months later, I received a letter. "My name is Cindy Davis," I read. "I'm your husband's lung recipient. Thank you for giving me life. . . . I'll always be grateful." *Oh, Gary!* I wept. *You did something wonderful!*

I wrote back telling her I was glad she was feeling better. Then Cindy wrote again, asking about Gary. What was he like?

"Gary was a good father, a generous friend and a loving husband," I answered. "He loved to make me laugh, but he was romantic, too."

Soon, we were corresponding, and sharing Cindy's letters with the boys eased some of our pain.

Still, I cried every day. And on what would have been our fifteenth anniversary, I placed roses on Gary's grave. Every year, he'd given me a bouquet of roses, but now all I had were memories. "I miss you!" I wept.

I went home, my grief nearly as raw as the day Gary died.

Early that evening, the doorbell rang. It was a delivery of roses. But from whom? Then I read the card: Happy Anniversary from Cindy. "What a wonderful thing to do!" I cried.

Later that same evening the phone rang. "I'm Gary Myers, your husband's heart recipient," a man said. He explained that he and Cindy had been in touch, and when she told him what day this was, he thought it was the right time to thank me.

The roses, the phone call, the comforting warmth I suddenly felt—it was as if Gary were behind it all, enveloping me in a hug.

And when Cindy called a few days later and asked if we could meet, I replied, "Yes!"

After a three-hour drive, the boys and I arrived at the courthouse where Cindy worked—and were greeted by a room filled with people and a banner that read, "Welcome Sandy, Jerrod and Casey."

Touched, I noticed a woman standing nearby. Somehow I just knew. "Cindy!" I cried, falling into her arms. Then a man walked over and said, "I'm Gary Myers."

Minutes later, another man spoke up. "I'm Lee Morrison," he explained. "I received Gary's liver."

"I can't believe this!" I exclaimed to Cindy.

"I wanted you to see how much your gift has meant," she smiled.

As we heard how Gary's gift had saved lives, my heart

lifted. Jerrod and Casey beamed as they shared memories of their dad.

The following weekend, Gary Myers and his wife invited us to visit with them. Gary took the boys fishing, and we got to know his family. And I found myself asking Gary if it would be all right if I listened to his heart . . . my Gary's heart.

"Of course," he nodded.

I filled with warmth as I listened to the steady heartbeat that had filled me with love all the years of my marriage. And when the boys listened, their eyes sparkled.

In the moments of peace that followed, I realized that Gary's gift had not only saved the recipients' lives—it was saving ours, too.

That was five years ago, and since then, we've met the two men who received Gary's kidneys. Like the others, they've become like family to us.

Today, Jerrod is in the Marines and Casey is a high-school athlete. We remember Gary with smiles instead of tears. Seeing how strong and happy my sons have grown fills me with pride. I know Gary would be proud, too.

I'll always be grateful for the joy I have in my life—and for the five angels who helped me find it once again.

Sandy Allinder
As told to Dianne Gill
Previously appeared in Woman's World

THE FAMILY CIRCUS.   By Bil Keane

"If somebody dies in the hospital, angels move
them to the eternity ward."

Reprinted with permission from Bil Keane.

Choosing to Live

I'm one of the stars
I shall be living
In one of them
I shall be laughing
And so it shall be
As if the stars
were laughing
When you look
At the sky at night

Antoine de Saint-Exupéry

In March 1981 our nine-year-old daughter, Julie, was diagnosed with cancer. Our world was shattered. Fear and hope became permanent residents in our home. We found that laughter and tears could be partners, that family and friends could lighten the burdens, that we persevered and did what must be done because there was no other choice. Our children needed us.

Julie had always been a child who thought things over and then asked many questions. She was filled with smiles, determination, charm and bossiness. Her sister was her confidante and ally, and she adored her little brother. Julie talked constantly and could never keep a secret.

We, in turn, did not keep her cancer a secret. She knew everything. During the course of her treatments she assured us that the tumor was gone, and we shouldn't worry. With other patients, she tied her name and address to helium-filled balloons at Children's Hospital. Through an open window she'd watch her wish-filled balloons escape to the sky. Once, a card with a message was mailed back to her. She liked to imagine traveling with that balloon, sailing with the winds across Lake Michigan, and then being found high in the branches of a tree.

Julie basked in the attention that the whole town gave her. Friends, and then strangers who became friends, rallied around our oldest child. They offered helping hands and held numerous fund-raisers. We were overwhelmed by their kindness.

During the summer Julie went to One Step at a Time Camp for children with cancer. She came home telling stories, singing songs and cracking jokes. Camp was the greatest place.

At the end of October she and her dad jetted off to Florida on Dream Flite, an airplane filled with children who had cancer or leukemia. It was magical. Then, suddenly and without warning, her vision started slipping away. The doctors could do nothing, and by December this unexpected side effect of radiation therapy had permanently damaged her optic nerves. Julie was blind. She wept and raged against the darkness, telling us that it was ever so much harder than having cancer because she had to think about it all the time.

Our once voracious reader now listened to tapes and slowly learned braille. Ten years old, she resented the hovering adults and missed her independence. Eager to strike out on her own again, she took her white cane and tapped her way down the street to her best friend's house. She continued her activities with her Girl Scout troop, rode her tandem bicycle, sang in the school chorus and returned to camp in the summer.

Our outspoken daughter attended several meetings of a group of adults with cancer. She answered their questions, made them laugh and forced them to look inside themselves. We received letters from some of them, in awe of a child who refused to give up, who treasured the saying, "When it rains, look for the rainbow."

Julie spent Christmas and her eleventh birthday in the hospital, again experiencing treatment-related problems. Seizures began, then a coma. Tests showed atrophy of her brain. On a cold January night I voiced the unspeakable. I told our beloved child, mature beyond her years, that we understood her body was no longer healthy enough to keep her here. I spoke of the wonders of heaven, and told her that it was okay for her to let go and leave. She was assured that we would miss her and love her forever. Weeping, I added that whenever there was a rainbow she should sit on top of it, and then slide down and wave to us.

The following morning her two-year fight ended. Our Julie was gone. We were devastated. An autopsy showed that there was no tumor. She was correct in her belief that she had beaten her cancer. The cause of her death was delayed effects from radiation.

Many things have happened since Julie died that let us know she continues to be with us. We see rainbows or pieces of rainbows everywhere. We see them on cloudy days, rainy days, sunny days, inside and outside. We always wave.

Lori, Julie's sister, released a balloon to the skies, silently whispering that she needed a sign that Julie was all right. A month later I handed her the card that had arrived in the mail. She broke into a huge smile accompanied by tears and explained that the card being returned was her much-needed sign. I like to imagine sailing with that balloon for a visit to heaven.

We have realized that Julie influences others in ways that let us know she is still loving us. Nine months after she died I was shopping and discovered a Christmas ornament that had been made for 1983. It was an angel, sitting on a rainbow, waving. I'm sure someone thought it was their own idea. We knew better.

That same year I contacted an artist and asked if he could paint a picture of Julie. I was unaware of his usual fees, but he gently explained that he charged thousands of dollars to paint portraits. He did, however, ask us to leave several pictures of Julie and her scrapbook so that he could do a pencil sketch. He added that he was very busy and probably wouldn't be able to get to it for quite some time. Three months later the artist called and apologized for being unable to do the sketch. He continued, "Let me explain. I tried to do the pencil sketch. It just wouldn't remain a sketch. Julie demanded to be painted. This has never happened to me before. It was as though someone else was painting through me. I feel like I know her; I was filled with happiness every time I worked on the portrait. I've stopped trying to understand what happened."

When my husband and I walked into his studio we became motionless, staring at the likeness of our daughter. Tears slid down our cheeks. We managed to tell the worried artist that nothing was wrong. The painting was beautiful. Our memories of Julie were filled with the past two years, with sickness. This portrait was of a healthy, happy child. He had picked up his brush and found her soul. His gift to us was even more than the portrait itself. He gave us peace.

Grief is a long, difficult journey. It consumed us, and it felt as though the anguish and pain would never end.

Heartbreak brought such emptiness, and her loss seemed unbearable. It was so wrong that a child should die. We kept wondering why and had to understand that some questions have no answers. There came a time during our suffering when we realized that we had to make a choice. It was our decision whether we should be bitter people or better people. In our daughter's memory, we chose to be better. We didn't want Julie to be forgotten. She enriched our lives and was still a part of us. Because she had been here, we were different than we would have been. We would have to become her legacy.

In 1985 our family returned to that summer camp for children with cancer. Julie was right—it was wonderful. We continue to volunteer there every July. I see children swimming, creating craft masterpieces, trekking up hills, singing around campfires, and my heart is warmed. I can hear my daughter's laughter in other children. It fills me with joy to see many of those campers grow up and become counselors. Others grow up in a place beyond my sight.

Julie continues to touch the lives of others through all of us who shared her brief time here on Earth. She travels with us into tomorrow.

People may die, but love never ends.

Chris Thiry

THE FAMILY CIRCUS.   By Bil Keane

". . . And if you find a purple balloon
up there, it's mine."

Reprinted with permission from Bil Keane.

The Mother Box

Late one December evening, bathed in the soft light of the Christmas tree, I lay on the couch with my eyes closed, letting my memories swirl around in pools of thought. Returning to the present, I opened my eyes and immediately my gaze fell upon a beautiful miniature Christmas city that lined my fireplace mantel. Well, it was really only half a city, as my dad had divided it between my sister and me twenty-five years earlier after our mother had passed away.

Little twinkle lights glowed from behind red cellophane windows in the tiny cardboard houses that had lined the living-room bookshelves of my childhood.

With no warning, the words tumbled out like a spilled glass of aged wine—words that had been hidden in my heart a long time, waiting to surface, "Mom, I miss you so much."

An ocean of tears ebbed and flowed for nearly an hour, and then the idea emerged. If I felt this way then surely my brother and sister did, too. Twenty-five years, five senses, one box—that's what I would do—I would capture the essence of my mother and place her in a box—a Mother Box—one for each of her children.

I began to think of our mother in terms of what scent

encompassed her, what look best described her, what sound echoed "Mother," and so on.

Including my ten-year-old daughter, Shiloah, in my quest, we searched to put together pieces of a grand-mother she'd never met.

First came the box all the memories would be housed in. Such a vast display we found. Flowered ones of every type ever found in a garden, ones with stars on them, moons, old-fashioned Victorian images, hearts and ones with Christmas themes, and then we saw them—angels! Yes, for a mother no longer of this Earth, it was perfect. But, there were only two. One sister, one brother—I'd make one for myself another time.

Oddly enough, the entire day was like that. We'd find two of just what we needed, no more, no less. With mounting excitement we took our treasures home and wrapped them with great love.

A river of memories wound its way through a thickly wooded forest of words, painting a picture of a thousand yesterdays, growing straight and tall like new seedlings among the old growth. Sealed with a simple envelope, they awaited their intended.

Just the right time presented itself to give my brother his box. As his eyes fell upon its contents, this man of thirty-seven was reduced to tears. My father was standing there, and I'll never forget the faraway look on his face. The years were melting away with each item my brother lifted from the Mother Box.

A package of grits representing a woman who grew up in the South and served it to her children for breakfast in Oregon—her favorite Johnny Mathis music—a shiny silver Christmas bow that felt like the party dresses she wore—a single silk red rose representing dozens my father had given her. I included the famous story of how once when they were courting he brought long-stemmed roses that were as long as he was tall! She adored red roses. Finally, a bottle of her favorite perfume, Emeraude. I could hardly believe they still made it, but there it was, that familiar green. The shape of the bottle had changed over the years, but when I sprayed the misty fragrance into the air, it was unmistakably the scent of our mother.

This journey of the heart, traveled with my daughter, brought us together in spirit. We were both bound with the cords of love from the life of a woman long gone, yet still sewn tightly in the memory quilt of our minds. We saw the continuing thread of life reflected in each other's eyes.

Then my daughter handed me a box. Inside was the essence of my mother—the fragrance of another generation reached out to touch her legacy. I opened the perfume bottle and sprayed, and she surrounded us.

Linda Webb Gustafson

Evolution

Grief is a most peculiar thing; we're so helpless in the face of it. It's like a window that will simply open of its own accord. The room grows cold, and we can do nothing but shiver. But, it opens a little less each time, and a little less; and one day we wonder what has become of it.

Arthur Golden

In the beginning, I walked around wringing my hands constantly like Lady Macbeth. Now I still wring them, but only on the anniversary of the hours leading up to her death and when hearing tragic news.

In the beginning, the videotape in my head played the events of the days before and after her death again and again. I was powerless to stop it. Now I can frequently turn it off by consciously thinking of other things.

In the beginning, I felt that my skin was too tight for my body. Compulsively, I had to move in order to make it fit. I walked for long periods in order to feel comfortable. Now I walk just for exercise.

In the beginning, on Tuesdays leading up to 12:25 P.M., I

tensely counted the minutes. Now Tuesday is usually just an ordinary day.

In the beginning, time was counted in days and weeks. Now it's numbered in years.

In the beginning, everything that belonged or related to her was sacred. When the earrings she had given me fell out, I was frantic. Now if they were lost, I would be very sad but I could cope. Now I donate many of the things she owned.

In the beginning, it was hard to think or talk about anything but her death. Now I have reinvested in life, have other topics of conversation and actually find much of life enjoyable.

In the beginning I cried when I passed her favorite foods in the supermarket. Now there is a pang but the tears no longer flow.

In the beginning, the words to "Wind Beneath My Wings" and "Somewhere Out There" echoed painfully in my head for months. Now when I hear those songs there is sadness, but it is softer and ends quickly.

In the beginning, I was sure I was crazy. Now, although I still question my sanity at times, I accept the fact that my thoughts and feelings are normal for bereaved parents.

In the beginning there were many things I wouldn't do. Now I do some of them but still avoid others. Perhaps in my continued evolution, I will decide those things are possible, too.

If you are at the beginning, take heart. There is evolution.

Stephanie Hesse

Who Is Jack Canfield?

Jack Canfield is one of America's leading experts in the development of human potential and personal effectiveness. He is both a dynamic, entertaining speaker and a highly sought-after trainer. Jack has a wonderful ability to inform and inspire audiences toward increased levels of self-esteem and peak performance.

He is the author and narrator of several bestselling audio- and videocassette programs, including *Self-Esteem and Peak Performance, How to Build High Self-Esteem, Self-Esteem in the Classroom* and *Chicken Soup for the Soul—Live.* He is regularly seen on television shows such as *Good Morning America, 20/20* and *NBC Nightly News.* Jack has co-authored numerous books, including the *Chicken Soup for the Soul* series, *Dare to Win* and *The Aladdin Factor* (all with Mark Victor Hansen), *100 Ways to Build Self-Concept in the Classroom* (with Harold C. Wells), *Heart at Work* (with Jacqueline Miller) and *The Power of Focus* (with Les Hewitt and Mark Victor Hansen).

Jack is a regularly featured speaker for professional associations, school districts, government agencies, churches, hospitals, sales organizations and corporations. His clients have included the American Dental Association, the American Management Association, AT&T, Campbell's Soup, Clairol, Domino's Pizza, GE, ITT, Hartford Insurance, Johnson & Johnson, the Million Dollar Roundtable, NCR, New England Telephone, Re/Max, Scott Paper, TRW and Virgin Records. Jack is also on the faculty of Income Builders International, a school for entrepreneurs.

Jack conducts an annual eight-day Training of Trainers program in the areas of self-esteem and peak performance. It attracts educators, counselors, parenting trainers, corporate trainers, professional speakers, ministers and others interested in developing their speaking and seminar-leading skills.

For further information about Jack's books, tapes and training programs, or to schedule him for a presentation, please contact:

Self-Esteem Seminars
P.O. Box 30880
Santa Barbara, CA 93130
phone: 805-563-2935 • fax: 805-563-2945
Web site: *www.chickensoup.com*

Who Is Mark Victor Hansen?

Mark Victor Hansen is a professional speaker who, in the last twenty years, has made over four thousand presentations to more than two million people in thirty-three countries. His presentations cover sales excellence and strategies; personal empowerment and development; and how to triple your income and double your time off.

Mark has spent a lifetime dedicated to his mission of making a profound and positive difference in people's lives. Throughout his career, he has inspired hundreds of thousands of people to create a more powerful and purposeful future for themselves while stimulating the sale of billions of dollars worth of goods and services.

Mark is a prolific writer and has authored *Future Diary*, *How to Achieve Total Prosperity* and *The Miracle of Tithing*. He is the coauthor of the *Chicken Soup for the Soul* series, *Dare to Win* and *The Aladdin Factor* (all with Jack Canfield) and *The Master Motivator* (with Joe Batten).

Mark has also produced a complete library of personal empowerment audio- and videocassette programs that have enabled his listeners to recognize and better use their innate abilities in their business and personal lives. His message has made him a popular television and radio personality with appearances on ABC, NBC, CBS, HBO, PBS, QVC and CNN.

He has also appeared on the cover of numerous magazines, including *Success, Entrepreneur* and *Changes*.

Mark is a big man with a heart and a spirit to match—an inspiration to all who seek to better themselves.

For further information about Mark, please contact:

Mark Victor Hansen & Associates
P.O. Box 7665
Newport Beach, CA 92658
phone: 949-759-9304 or 800-433-2314
fax: 949-722-6912
Web site: *www.chickensoup.com*

Contributors

Sandy Allinder received her associate of arts degree from Wallace State Community College, Hanceville, Alabama, in 1992 and her bachelor of science degree from the University of Montevallo, Alabama, in December 1994. She currently teaches fifth grade at Hayden Middle School in Blount County, Alabama. Please reach her at *sandyexp@bellsouth.net.*

Barbara Bergen is a former history teacher who retired in 1996 to become a writer. Her writings have appeared in *Unity Magazine* and *Daily Word Prayer Journal.* She creates and sells inspirational cards, bookmarks and books. Other interests include photography, travel and collecting quotes. Please reach her at *BarbBergen@aol.com.*

Mike Bergen worked as a sports correspondent for the *Atlantic City Press* and several local radio stations while attending Stockton State College. Today he is the vice president of a large millwork supplier in Vineland, New Jersey. A research fund has been established in Mikey's memory at the Medical College of Virginia. Contributions can be sent to: MCV Foundation—Michael W. Bergen Fund, P.O. Box 980234, Richmond, VA 23298.

Janelle M. Breese Biagioni lives with her family in Victoria, British Columbia. She has written several books, including *Head Injuries: The Silent Epidemic* (NC Press, 1995), a personal accounting following her husband's police motorcycle accident in which he sustained a severe brain injury. For more information on Janelle, please view her Web site at *www.soulwriter.com.*

Linda Bremner is a mother and grandmother, although her business card reads, "Founder and Executive Director" of Love Letters, Inc. At fifty-five, she has been involved with the art community, especially paper crafts, for over thirty-five years. She has had several articles published and is also a lecturer and motivational speaker. To make a tax-deductible contribution to Love Letters, Inc., or to find out about volunteering, please contact Linda at: P.O. Box 416875, Chicago, IL 60641 or at the Web site *www.lovelettersinc.org.*

Connie Sturm Cameron is a freelance writer who resides in Glenford, Ohio, with her husband, Chuck, and two teenagers, Chase and Chelsea. She has been published in several periodicals, including *Reader's Digest* and *The Upper Room.* You may contact her at P.O. Box 30, Glenford, OH 43739 or e-mail *conniec@netpluscom.com.*

Kevin D. Catton has remarried and, with his wife Jeri-Lynn, operates The Log House Bed & Breakfast on fifty forested acres in St. Jacobs, Amish Country, about an hour west of Toronto. Visit them at *www.theloghouse.on.ca* or e-mail *info@theloghouse.on.ca.*

Hana Haatainen Caye is a freelance writer and an independent contractor, working as a certified business consultant, inspector, auditor, investigator and actress. She is married with two daughters (ages eighteen and twenty) and enjoys studying her Bible, gardening, horseback riding, entertaining, decorating and caring for her menagerie of pets. She has published poetry and magazine articles and is currently working on several children's books. She won an award for her writing in 1975.

Candy Chand, along with Kathleen Treanor, is the author of the book, *Ashley's Garden*, available in bookstores nationwide.

Jo Coudert is a freelance writer, a frequent contributor to *Woman's Day* and the author of eight books, among them the bestselling *Advice from a Failure* and *Seven Cats and the Art of Living*. She lives on the bank of a small river in western New Jersey, where she gardens and paints.

Robert P. Curry is a graduate of Eastern Washington University and works for the Department of the Navy. He spent four years in Japan while in the United States Marine Corps. Robert enjoys writing and spending time with his teenage daughter. He is currently working on a children's book and inspirational novel. Please reach him at *nahaman001@aol.com*.

Amanda Dodson is a full-time mother to two beautiful children, Grace and Garrett. She is a freelance writer and is at work on her first children's book.

Dr. Ken Druck, founder and executive director of The Jenna Druck Foundation in San Diego, California, is an author *(How to Talk to Your Kids About School Violence* and *The Secrets Men Keep)*, consulting psychologist and inspirational speaker. The Foundation's Families Helping Families program *(www. jennadruck.org)* offers free programs and services to families who have experienced the death of a child. Dr. Druck has been working extensively in New York with fire department and civilian families who lost loved ones in the September 11, 2001 terrorist attacks.

Kara L. Dutchover lives in Oregon with her husband of twenty-one years, Hank, and their three children. She credits the sweet chaos of family life, ornery pets and a loving God for any truth or power in her writing.

Aaron Espy, firefighter/paramedic, is a twenty-one-year fire service veteran. He has authored a book of firehouse poetry titled, *Standing in the Gap*, a 911 column for the *Scripps-Howard West Sound Sun*, and numerous inspirational articles. He can be reached at *AARONESPY@prodigy.net*.

Janice Finnell is a freelance writer and winner of a Lowell Thomas Award for exceptional journalism. She lives in New Jersey with her husband, Ian, and two sons, Gabe, three, and D.J., one. Janice is currently working on her first book, a middle-grade novel. She can be reached at *jlfinnell@aol.com*.

Michael Gartner, principal owner of the Iowa Cubs baseball team, has been the editor of newspapers large and small and president of *NBC News*. In 1997, he won the Pulitzer Prize for editorial writing.

Dianne Gill is a writer for *Woman's World* magazine. She has two grown children and resides in Long Island, New York, with her husband, Steve. In her spare time she enjoys gardening, photography, and entertaining family and friends. She feels honored to have written so many human-interest stories about people who have persevered in the face of challenge. Her e-mail address is *diwriter@optonline.net*.

Gloria Givens is a California freelance journalist published in both magazines and newspapers. Her husband, Ken, died after forty-two years of marriage, so her writing reflects life experiences and her faith in a better tomorrow. She enjoys camping with her four children, eight grandchildren, friends and pets. E-mail: *g4givens@Yahoo.com*.

Linda Webb Gustafson finds inspiration for stories from her life experiences in Village Missions, where she ministers with her husband, David, and children, Shiloah and Joshua, in Skamania, Washington. Her work has been included in two national Christian publications and community newspapers such as the award-winning *Cannon Beach Gazette*. You can e-mail Linda at *vmwordsmith@yahoo.com* or write her at P.O. Box 443, North Bonneville, WA 98639. Her phone number is 509-427-8517.

Ruth Hancock has been published in magazines, hospice journals, books, including *Chicken Soup for the Volunteer's Soul,* and newspapers writing short stories based on her life and interests. They include hospice volunteer, wife of an Episcopal priest, mother, a long career in the fashion industry as a model, fashion director and commentator, and as a dedicated Christian. She can be reached by e-mail at *Rahancock@worldnet.att.net*.

Emily Sue Harvey's upbeat stories appear in women's magazines, *Chocolate for a Woman's Spirit, Chocolate for a Woman's Soul, Chicken Soup for the Soul* publications and in the anthology, *From Eulogy to Joy.* Her current project is a fictional novel about the struggles of an all-too-human preacher's family, entitled *God Only Knows.* Please contact her at 864-879-2733 or e-mail *EmilySue1@aol.com*.

Joyce A. Harvey is a motivational and inspirational speaker, trainer, facilitator and writer. Watch for her forthcoming books: *Swan Lessons,* the story of her journey through grief; *I'm Fine—I'm with the Angels,* an illustrated children's book on dying and life after death; and *Traveling Swan Lessons: Mystical and Magical Road Stories,* a collection of her magical encounters while traveling. For further information about Ms. Harvey or to schedule her for a presentation, please contact her at P.O. Box 160, Sylvania, OH 43560. Fax: 419-885-9469. E-mail: *Harveback@aol.com*.

Bill Heavey is a freelance writer in Arlington, Virginia, who writes about people, travel, food, the outdoors and other things that move him. He can be reached at *bheavey@erols.com*.

Nina A. Henry is the devoted mother of two sons, Adam and Ryan. Her oldest son, Adam, died suddenly and unexpectedly in 1996. She and her husband,

Charles, are founding members of the Peace Valley Chapter of Compassionate Friends located in New Britain, Pennsylvania. She can be contacted at *nhenry@cbsd.org*.

Stephanie Hesse became a bereaved parent in 1994 when twenty-seven-year-old Linda died. She, Peter and Carol miss Linda immensely. Stephanie is an active member of The Compassionate Friends, a support group for grieving families. She is a retired reading teacher who, as a volunteer, teaches reading skills to third-graders. Stephanie lives in Chestnut Ridge, New York, and Singer Island, Florida.

Dawn Holt is currently a school counselor at Westover High School in Fayetteville, North Carolina, fulfilling her son Cameron's last wishes that he not be forgotten and that she come back to his high school to make a difference in the lives of the students. After giving the chocolate-covered cherries story to family and friends in December 1998, they encouraged her to submit the story to *Chicken Soup for the Soul*. She still makes the box of candy her annual gift to them. Please e-mail Dawn at *dawnholt@yahoo.com*.

Bill Holton is a freelance writer living in Gainesville, Florida. He can be reached at *bholton@reporters.net*.

Ann Hood is the author of seven novels including *Somewhere Off the Coast of Maine, Places to Stay at Night* and *Ruby*, and one non-fiction book, *Do Not Go Gentle: My Search for Miracles in a Cynical Time*. She lives in Providence, Rhode Island. Her story, "Missing Pa," originally appeared in *Parenting Magazine*.

Molly Bruce Jacobs practiced corporate law prior to becoming a full-time writer. She has published short stories and essays in numerous literary journals and popular magazines. Originally from Maryland, she now lives outside of Santa Fe, New Mexico, where she is writing a non-fiction book. You may reach her at *m.b.jacobs@att.net*.

Bil Keane created *The Family Circus* in 1960 and gathered most of his ideas from his own family: wife Thel and their five children. Now read by an estimated 188 million people daily, nine grandchildren provide much of the inspiration for the award-winning feature. Web site: *www.familycircus.com*.

Cynthia G. Kelley's poem was published in the January 1988 issue of *Bereavement* magazine. *Bereavement, a magazine of hope and healing* is dedicated to serving those who are grieving the death of a loved one. Based in Colorado Springs, Colorado, their toll-free phone number is 888-604-4673 and their Web page is *www.bereavementmag.com*.

Natalie "Paige" Kelly-Lunceford is a mother, grandmother and foster mother. She lives in a quiet rural area of Virginia with her husband of twenty-four years, Tracy. She enjoys children and has taken in more than thirty over the last thirteen years, in addition to having four children and two grandchildren of her own. She enjoys reading and writing short articles and poems. Please e-mail her at *natalies40@hotmail.com*.

Barb Kerr wrote this story in memory of her nephew, Joe Goodfellow. She has two sons, Matthew and Shawn, a niece, Heather and two nephews Edward and Chris. She loves celebrating life with them all. She is a certified financial planner in Parry Sound, Ontario, Canada. You may reach her at *attacklife4@ hotmail.com.*

Ed and **Sandra Kervin** reside in Albion, Maine. Both are active volunteers for the Hospice Volunteers Organization. As they continue their journey through life as grieving parents, they have refocused their efforts on their surviving children, Lori and Adam. Even in death, their son and brother, Jarod, continues to have a positive effect on others, as evidenced by their contribution to this book and the work they continue to do with Suicide Education. They can be reached at *oldcrows@midmaine.com.*

Monica Kiernan received her B.A. in health education and certification in physical therapy from California State University, Northridge in 1992. She now practices in New Hampshire where she resides with her husband. Jack, and their son, Jackson, and daughter, Kelsea, who continue to amuse, delight and inspire her each day.

Ferne Kirshenbaum was a wife, mother, grandmother and high-school English teacher. She died of ovarian cancer in 1998.

Allen Klein's story, "Two Answers to One Prayer," is from his book, *The Courage to Laugh.* He is an award-winning professional speaker, as well as the author of *The Healing Power of Humor.* Reach him via e-mail at *humor@allenklein.com* or on his Web site at *www.allenklein.com.*

Kathie Kroot lives with her family in Kentucky. She remains an active volunteer in her children's school and at her synagogues. She continues to promote organ donation, especially within the Jewish community. You can read her articles on the subject at *www.transweb.org.* You can reach her at *kvk4660@aol.com.*

Kelly E. Kyburz and her husband, Jeff, live in Collegeville, Pennsylvania, with their three daughters and two sons. They are both majors in the U.S. Army Reserve. Kelly graduated from Loyola College (Baltimore) with a degree in finance and earned an M.B.A. from Indiana University. Her sister, LTC Kathy Gilmartin, graduated from West Point and is currently serving in the U.S. Army. Her brother, Chris Cain, is living his dream as a firefighter in Maryland. Their parents, John and Marcella Cain, were happily married for thirty-six years. E-mail Kelly at *Kellyk@itiaccess.com.*

Richard Lepinsky became a bereaved parent in May 1991 when son Nathan died of viral pneumonia. He became involved in The Compassionate Friends, a bereaved parent support group. Richard is a former business owner and vice president of the Compassionate Friends of Canada. Please reach him at *www.ForNathan.com.*

Scott Michael Mastley, S.P.M.R., is a surviving sibling and a powerful writer and speaker. His book, *Surviving a Sibling,* fills a gap in grief literature by specifically addressing the unique aspects of sibling grief. Visit his Web site at *www.survivingasibling.com* for book information, links and e-mail, or write to The Box Press, P.O. Box 1925, Suwanee, GA 30024.

Linda Maurer graduated from Stephens College in 1962. She and Larry were married in 1969 and reside in Colorado. Her books can be obtained through bookstores or through the Centering Corporation in Omaha, Nebraska. She can be reached at P.O. Box 1638, Nederland, CO 80466.

Walker Meade began to write stories at the age of fourteen. When he was twenty-two, one of his pieces was published in *Colliers* magazine. He then wrote short fiction for the *Saturday Evening Post, Good Housekeeping* and *Gentleman's Quarterly,* among others. He then turned to writing nonfiction for magazines such as *Cosmopolitan, Reader's Digest* and *Redbook.* Later he became the managing editor of *Cosmopolitan* and then the managing editor of *Reader's Digest Condensed Book Club.* His last position in publishing was as president and editor in chief of Avon Books. Today he is retired and concentrates on writing longer fiction. Upstart Press published his first novel in August 2001. It has had exciting critical reception and is selling unusually well. The book, *Unspeakable Acts,* can be ordered from *Amazon.com.*

Ted Menten has been visiting children in hospitals for nearly a decade. He also volunteers to help terminally ill children, adults and their families. This year Running Press Book Publishers (*www.runningpress.com*) will release two new Ted Menten books: *Gentle Closings, Second Edition* and *The Gentle Closings Question and Answer Book.*

Cindy Midgette lives in eastern North Carolina with her husband, Buddy, and children, Brent and Allie. Cindy is an avid animal lover. She supports Airedale rescue: *www.airedale.org.* Please contact her at *Bonnie@pamlico.com.*

Diane C. Nicholson is a freelance writer and award-winning photographer living in British Columbia's North Okanagan. She and her family own Nicholson Prints, selling photo art prints and limited edition prints, specializing in horses and companion animals, through their Web site at *www.twinheartphoto.com* or by phone at 250-546-2560.

Bob Perks is a professional speaker, vocalist and author of *The Flight of a Lifetime!* Visit *www.iwishyouenough.com* for his weekly messages, "I Believe in You!" Contact him at *Bob@BobPerks.com* or P.O. Box 1702, Shavertown, PA 18708-1702.

Debi L. Pettigrew graduated magna cum laude from Central State University, Edmond, Oklahoma. She currently works as the marketing director for the DME Company. She resides in Melbourne, Florida, and writes articles, poetry and prose on grief-related and inspirational subjects. She is available for freelance work and can be reached at 321-254-5440 or via e-mail at *dlpettigrew@msn.com.*

Rachel Naomi Remen, M.D., is clinical professor of family and community medicine at UCSF School of Medicine, and director and founder of the Institute for the Study of Health and Illness at Commonweal. She is the author of *Kitchen Table Wisdom* and *My Grandfather's Blessings*. For more information, please visit *www.rachelremen.com.*

Lark Whittemore Ricklefs has not been published before. After losing "Jen," she wrote to heal her broken heart and maybe help other grieving parents. She thanks God for sending a dragonfly that has appeared to her many times. Lark told her sixth graders at Seton in Algona the story, and the same day she received the letter from *Chicken Soup for the Grieving Soul*. What a special honor to know that "Jen" will be remembered forever. Lark can be reached at 814 South Harriet, Algona, IA 50511 or at her e-mail address *larktjjen@yahoo.com.*

Sarah A. Rivers is a Salem College graduate and a non-resident member of the Junior League of Charlotte, North Carolina. Her interests lie in writing inspirational poetry and nonfiction articles for publication. She and her husband, Ralph, live in Dallas, Texas. Sarah can be reached at 214-503-0195.

Doris Sanford is a registered nurse with a Ph.D. in counseling psychology. She has taught a college course in death and dying for the past thirty years and authored twenty-nine books for or about children. She provides seminars worldwide on meeting the needs of abused children. Please reach her at *d.e.sanford@att.net.*

Jim Schneegold is a legal printer in Cheektowaga, New York (suburb of Buffalo) who writes heartfelt personal-experience stories spanning from childhood embarrassments to late yesterday. His contributions to *Chicken Soup for the Soul* are a representation of his family values and a personal contribution to all who may benefit from them. He can be reached at 630 Beach Road, Cheektowaga, NY 14225 or via e-mail at *goldensnow@aol.com.*

Maria E. Sears is enjoying an active retirement. In addition to writing, she keeps busy with multiple volunteer organizations, traveling with her husband, doing numerous crafts and spending time with her two granddaughters. She can be reached by e-mail at *deriter@aol.com.*

Duane Shearer is a busy, stay-at-home wife and mom with her seven-year-old, Savannah Swinehart. She had a second kidney transplant in June 2001 thanks to her husband Bob Swinehart's generous donation of one of his kidneys. The family is doing great.

Robin Lee Shope has nearly one hundred magazine articles in print. She is a teacher and lives with her husband and their two children near Dallas, Texas.

Chris Thiry is a teacher's assistant for children with learning disabilities in Grayslake, Illinois. She is married and has three children; two have grown up in this world, and one has traveled beyond. She hopes that her story will bring comfort to those who grieve. Chris and her family continue to volunteer their time every summer at the One Step at a Time Camp for children with cancer. For information please visit their Web site at *www.onestepcamp.org* or call 847-439-2127.

Dr. Roger William Thomas is the senior minister of First Christian Church in Vandalia, Missouri. A native of McLean County, Illinois, Roger is a preacher, author, Bible teacher, conference speaker, father of three and grandfather of four. He is a graduate of Lincoln Christian College and Seminary in Lincoln, Illinois. His doctorate is from Northern Baptist Theological Seminary. Roger may be contacted at 205 W. Park St., Vandalia, MO 63382.

Katherine Von Ahnen writes juvenile historic fiction and has four books published targeted on the Cape May, New Jersey, Lighthouse and Native-Americans. She was named New Jersey Poet of the Year in 1997. She resides at her Florida Quarter-Horse Equestrian Training Center. Reach her at *sue@s-bar-j.com.*

Steve Wilson, C.S.P., joyologist, psychologist, author and speaker, is founder of the World Laughter Tour, Inc., leading the world to health, happiness and peace through laughter clubs. He teaches people around the world how to stay healthy and prevent hardening of the attitudes. A top-rated speaker, Steve can be reached at *www.laughterclubs.com* or 1-800-NOW-LAFF.

Paul D. Wood, a resident of Maui for three decades, taught for many years on the faculty of Seabury Hall, a college-prep secondary school. He now works as an independent writer-for-hire. His most recent published book is a collection of stories called *False Confessions* (see *www.falseconfessions.com*).

Permissions

We would like to acknowledge the many publishers and individuals who granted us permission to reprint the cited material. (Note: The stories that were penned anonymously, that are in the public domain, or that were written by Jack Canfield or Mark Victor Hansen are not included in this listing.)

A Timeless Gift. Reprinted by permission of Gloria Givens. ©2001 Gloria Givens.

A Rose for Mother. Reprinted by permission of Maria E. Sears. ©2000 Maria E. Sears.

Mom's Last Laugh. Reprinted by permission of Robin Lee Shope. ©1999 Robin Lee Shope.

I'm Okay, Mom and Dad. Reprinted by permission of Lark Whittemore Ricklefs. ©1997 Lark Whittemore Ricklefs.

Meant to Be. Reprinted by permission of Cindy Midgette. ©1999 Cindy Midgette.

A Surprise Gift for Mother. Reprinted by permission of Sarah A. Rivers. ©1997 Sarah A. Rivers.

A Gift of Faith. Reprinted by permission of Kelly E. Kyburz. ©2002 Kelly E. Kyburz.

I'll Make You a Rainbow. Reprinted by permission of Linda Bremner. ©2000 Linda Bremner.

Seven White, Four Red, Two Blue. Reprinted by permission of Robert P. Curry. ©1999 Robert P. Curry.

Joseph's Living Legacy. Reprinted by permission of Kathie Kroot and Bill Holton. ©2000 Kathie Kroot and Bill Holton. Appeared in *Woman's World;* Issue October, 2000.

To Remember Me. Reprinted by permission of Andrew W. Test. ©Robert N. Test.

The Pencil Box. Reprinted by permission of Doris Sanford. ©1997 Doris Sanford.

When No Words Seem Appropriate. By permission of Ann Landers and Creators Syndicate, Inc.

What You Can Do for a Grieving Friend. Copyright ©1988 by Jo Coudert. First published in *Woman's Day.* Reprinted by permission of The Richard Parks Agency.

Lot's Wife. By Rachel Naomi Remen, M.D., from *My Grandfather's Blessings* by Rachel Naomi Remen, M.D., copyright ©2000 by Rachel Naomi Remen, M.D. Used by permission of Riverhead Books, a division of Penguin Putnam, Inc.

One So Young. Reprinted by permission of Diane C. Nicholson. ©2000